Marxist Left Review

Number 28 – Summer 2024

Editor
Omar Hassan

Editorial committee
Mick Armstrong
Sandra Bloodworth
Omar Hassan
Louise O'Shea
Jordan Humphreys

Reviews editor
Alexis Vassiley

© Social Research Institute

Published by Socialist Alternative
Melbourne, December 2024

PO Box 4354
Melbourne University, VIC 3052

www.marxistleftreview.org

marxistleftreview@gmail.com

Contributions to *Marxist Left Review* are peer-reviewed

ISSN 1838-2932
rrp. $20

Subediting and proofreading
Tess Lee Ack
Diane Fieldes

Layout and production
Susan Miller

Cover
"Dangerous Red II: Palestine",
Marty Hirst, 2024, acrylic on stretched canvas.

Printed by IngramSpark

Marxist Left Review is a theoretical journal published twice-yearly by Socialist Alternative, a revolutionary organisation based in Australia.

We aim to engage with theoretical and political debates on the Australian and international left, making a rigorous yet accessible case for Marxist politics. We also seek to provide analysis of the social, political and economic dynamics shaping Australian capitalism.

Unless indicated otherwise all articles published reflect the views of the individual author(s).

We rely on our readers' support to continue publication.
You can help by subscribing at
marxistleftreview.org

mlr
Marxist Left Review

Number 28 Summer 2024

Editor
Sandra Bloodworth

Editorial committee
Mick Armstrong
Sandra Bloodworth
Omar Hassan
Louise O'Shea
Jordan Humphreys

Reviews editor
Vashti Kenway

Federal Reserve Institution

Published by Socialist Alternative
Melbourne, December 2024

PO Box 7274
Melbourne University, Vic 3052

www.marxistleftreview.org
marxistleftreview@gmail.com

Subscriptions: four issues
Regular/Low paid/Solidarity

ISSN 1836-X?
pp. 220

Typesetting and proofreading

Layout and production
Justin M. ?

Cover

Printed by Hagraphics

Marxist Left Review is a theoretical journal published twice-yearly by Socialist Alternative, a revolutionary organisation based in Australia.

We aim to engage with theoretical and political debates on the Australian and international left, making a rigorous and accessible case for Marxist politics. We also seek to provide analysis of the social, political and economic dynamics shaping Australian capitalism.

Unless otherwise stated, articles published mirror the views of the individual author(s).

We rely on our readers' support to continue publication. You can help by subscribing at marxistleftreview.org

Marxist Left Review　　　　Number 28 – Summer 2024

FEATURES

1　OWEN MARSDEN-READFORD
　　The United Nations is no friend of the Palestinians

27　NICK EVERETT
　　Labor's long embrace with apartheid Israel

63　TOM BRAMBLE
　　Empty promises: the ANC's failure to
　　deliver freedom in South Africa

111　APRIL HOLCOMBE
　　Let a hundred flowers wither: the many
　　failures of Western Maoism

145　MATT LAIDLAW
　　Why the Kenyan youth revolted:
　　interview with a Kenyan socialist

REVIEWS

163　APRIL HOLCOMBE
　　Review: China in global capitalism

179　LUCA TAVAN
　　Review: Zombie Kautskyism

197　MATT LAIDLAW
　　Review: The hidden history of
　　revolutionary politics in Africa

mlr

OWEN MARSDEN-READFORD

The United Nations is no friend of the Palestinians

Owen Marsden-Readford is a socialist activist based in Wollongong.

ISRAEL'S GENOCIDAL WAR on Gaza has made a mockery of international law. The Israeli military violates the supposed "rules of war" daily. Several articles and additional protocols in the Geneva Conventions give protection to children caught in armed conflict. Israel ratified the Geneva Conventions in 1951. Under international law, it is bound to "[e]stablish hospitals and safety zones for children under 15... ensure access to essential foodstuffs, clothing and tonics for children in areas that are under siege", among other measures.[1]

Israel clearly has no concern for this. As of June, nearly 15,000 children are dead in Gaza, according to the United Nations Office of the High Commissioner of Human Rights. Another 21,000 children are missing. Nearly 300 aid workers have been killed since Israel began its genocide in Gaza, including at least 220 United Nations workers.

The United Nations has been rendered totally powerless. At the time of writing, Israel has just launched a war on Lebanon, an act of aggression justified by Israeli Prime Minister Benjamin Netanyahu during his recent address to the United Nations. A non-binding General Assembly motion earlier in September demanding Israel end "its unlawful presence in the Occupied Palestinian Territory" within

---

1. International Committee of the Red Cross 1949.

12 months has meant nothing. The impotency of the UN in the face of humanitarian crisis has been made obvious. The UN has been reduced to making pleading media statements.

This has seen increased criticism of the UN. The sickening hypocrisy of the worthy rhetoric of human rights and justice espoused by Western imperialist powers as they stand with Israel has brought more criticism of the international "rules-based order".

This is positive. Yet, much criticism of the UN still accepts the premise that the UN should and could play the role it claims for itself. Calls to reform the UN and make international law more stringent so it can live up to its professed values abound. These calls are at best utopian, but more generally can sow illusions in the UN or a different constellation of bourgeois states or international actors to intervene to save Palestine and punish Israel.

The UN's charter claims that it exists to "develop friendly relations among nations based on respect for the principle of equal rights and self-determination of peoples, and to take other appropriate measures to strengthen universal peace".[2] The structure and history of the UN and its intervention in Palestine prove the opposite.

International law and multilateral institutions like the UN are not checks and balances on imperialism. The UN is not a limited or flawed body striving for peace, but a political body, fundamentally constituted by imperialism and working in the interests of the dominant imperial powers. Calls to strengthen or reform the UN miss this vital point. It is part and parcel of the imperialist system responsible for Israel's genocide in Palestine. Even when the UN or other international institutions denounce war crimes or try to pressure a state to avoid a certain course of action, they do so not from the vantage point of opposing the structures of imperialism, but in an attempt to manage the outcome of the instability produced by the dynamics of imperialism.

---

2. United Nations 1945.

Imperialism and international law

The barbarity of Israel's actions and the particular support given by the West leads many to understand imperialism as simply the actions of particularly powerful states, primarily the United States and its allies. This understanding of imperialism as the result of the actions of particular governments lends itself to holding illusions in international law and the UN. Perhaps international law can be used to curb the most violent impulses of the worst states and rein in warmongers.

For example, Stuart Rees, an academic and pro-Palestine writer, wrote in a November article:

> That stance may offend the US and Israel, but international law and UN resolutions have universal application, they are not a pick and choose means of deciding that powerful nations can be judged exceptional, their brutalities ignored.
>
> Bolstered by that principle, The Responsibility to Protect, UN inaction over Palestine can be replaced by authorising a peace force to be sent to Israel.[3]

To the extent international law or the UN fails in this task, it is seen as a problem of efficacy. Some way of strengthening international law and its disciplining power should supposedly allow it to play the role it is meant to.

International law is incapable of taming the crimes of imperialism. This is because imperialism is not simply the product of the policy of particular governments and countries. It is, as Lenin termed it, "the latest phase of capitalism", where economic competition has grown over into political and military competition between states and their blocs of national capital. Imperialism is continually produced and reproduced by competition in the world economy. It is baked into the very nature of global capitalism.

International law grew up and exists on the basis of capitalist imperialism. Like other forms of bourgeois law, international law is an expression of capitalist social relations, not something existing in

---

3. Rees 2023.

opposition to it. The hypocrisies of international law – such as Israel's and the West's claim of the Israeli right to self-defence against the Palestinians – express the point of international law rather than its ineffectiveness. As the Marxist critic of international law China Miéville argues, it should be understood to be

> an active part of conflictual international politics, used by states against each other. This is an international law which reflects and facilitates the interests of great powers in the international arena, rather than any autonomous legal sphere the careful application of which tends towards peace and justice.[4]

International law espouses a formal equality of rights. The reality of global politics is, however, one of inequality. There are powerful imperialist countries and weak nations. What could possibly adjudicate between two equal claims to rights under international law, say between both Israeli and Palestinian claims to the internationally recognised right to self-defence? As Marx wrote, "between equal rights force decides".[5] This force is imperialism and its hierarchy of state power. International law should be understood as an effective force. Its inability to hold strong nations to account as it can the weak expresses the unequal violence of the imperialist system in which international law exists. "Rogue nations" cannot be held to account by international law when those states are powerful imperialist countries like Israel and America.

In fact, this is part of what makes international law and the institutions that maintain it useful for the dominant imperialist powers. The hypocrisy of international law allows it to act as an effective force in the service of imperialism. International law is used as a tool of imperialist hegemony, to justify actions by imperialist nations and attempt to punish states which act against their interests. Wars waged by powers at the peak of the world pecking order, such as the United States' war and occupation of Afghanistan in 2001, are noble actions upholding international law, while similar invasions and wars of occupation, like

---

4. Miéville 2005, p.31.
5. Marx 1887.

Russia's invasion of Ukraine, are condemned as criminal violations of international law. When international law cannot be used as a tool to sanctify imperialist actions, it can be freely ignored.

As Miéville writes, international law is "complicit in the worst of today's social problems, and yet is fundamentally unreformable".[6]

Founding of the United Nations – a thieves kitchen

The UN itself, launched in 1945, is a creation of imperialism. Trotskyist Joseph Vanzler wrote at the time:

> It is calculated to counteract and to destroy any and all insurgent movements of the European peoples, above all Germany. It is aimed to perpetuate the existing inequality among nations rather than to establish any genuine equality among them.[7]

The UN was born as part of the jockeying for position between the United States, Russia and the United Kingdom, each seeking to maximise their position in the post-World War Two world order. By the end of that war, the US was the new dominant power. It boasted the world's largest military and economy. The US had aspirations for its industries, the most advanced and productive in the world, to penetrate the world economy through free trade.

For the Americans, the creation of the United Nations would have a number of uses.[8] First, the UN, alongside other international bodies in which the US predominated, would allow the US to use its muscle to hold back plans for economic blocs resistant to American pressure. Second, the founding of the UN allowed the US to write the rules for the postwar "rules-based order". Shaping and helping to construct the institutions of the postwar world served the US well. The UN was to be one such tool, alongside the IMF and the Bretton Woods exchange agreement. Initially, the UN was stacked with countries sympathetic to the US. A declaration of war on the Axis powers was required to join in

---

6. Miéville 2005, p.3.
7. Vanzler 1945.
8. Kolko 1990, p.242.

1945. By 1953, 800 resolutions had been passed in the General Assembly. The US got its way in 97 percent of these votes.[9]

America did have to compromise with other powers, primarily Russia and Britain, but America dominated the negotiations to set up the UN. Britain and Russia each sought to maintain their spheres of influence but understood that it was better to be part of the establishment of the UN than left in the cold. For a declining power like Britain, the sun setting on its days of imperial prestige, there was little choice anyway.

The structure, as well as the frequent powerlessness of the UN, reflect its imperial origins. From the negotiations emerged the United Nations, dominated by the Security Council with five permanent members reflecting the postwar balance of power: the US, Russia, Britain, France and China. While other countries rotate through the Security Council, the five permanent members retain veto power, ensuring that the UN is powerless against the interests of the major imperialist powers. Just one of the five states has to use its veto power and the UN is rendered impotent. America has used its veto power 49 times since the 1970s to protect Israel. The Security Council, the core of the UN, is, as the US State Department has said, dominated by "power politics, pure and simple".[10]

Veto power and the way it structurally entrenches the interests of the US and dominant imperialist powers is a feature, not a bug of the UN. The idea of a veto was not new in 1945. It was carried over from the structure of the League of Nations, the precursor to the UN. Lenin called the League a "thieves' kitchen". When the major powers agreed on subjugating a weak country, the League, like the UN, acted to justify this. If they disagreed, its rules could be happily ignored. In the League, the Council sat above the Assembly. Consisting of four permanent members and later nine members elected every three years, each member of the council held veto power. The structure of any such international body necessarily reflects the pecking order of imperialism. It is impossible for there to be some institution sitting above the power of the strongest states and acting as a neutral arbiter. Lenin said of the

---

9. Baxter 1999.
10. Kolko 1990, p.482.

League of Nations "that the alliance of the capitalist powers is sheer fraud, and that in actual fact it is an alliance of robbers, each trying to snatch something from the others".[11] This is equally true of the UN.

The UN General Assembly, for its part, is little more than a talk shop. As membership of the assembly increased throughout the twentieth century, more power was centralised in the hands of the Security Council. All UN military action has been authorised by the council since 1961. General Assembly resolutions are non-binding and symbolic, often just acting as rhetorical window dressing as the real games of imperial power happen elsewhere.

Powerlessness is not the problem – the history of UN and Palestine

A powerful United Nations, however, would not be a force for peace. Calls to strengthen the UN, or for it to "work", often gloss over the real history of UN intervention. When the UN does act, it seeks to smooth out the fraying edges of the world system in the interests of the dominant imperialist nations, not as a genuine force for peace. Nowhere is this clearer than in the history of UN intervention in Palestine. When the UN "works" it has meant further disaster for the Palestinians.

The partition of Palestine

One of the first acts of the United Nations was the partition of historic Palestine. In 1947, the UN turned over the question of Palestine to the United Nations Special Committee on Palestine, UNSCOP. Ignoring the demands of Palestinian representatives, this body rejected any notion that there could be a singular democratic state in Palestine. The carving up of Palestine so as to hand huge swathes of it to a minority Jewish population was practically taken for granted. UNSCOP was heavily influenced by the US and Russia. Both superpowers were strong supporters of the creation of a Zionist outpost in the Middle East. Each hoped that the new state would serve their interests in the postwar power struggle.

The UNSCOP report became the basis for General Assembly

---

11. Lenin 1966, p.323.

resolution 181, officially partitioning Palestine over the heads of the Palestinians themselves. How this sat alongside the principle of self-determination the UN rhetorically championed was never made clear. The resolution contained no means to prevent the ethnic cleansing of Palestine.

Israeli historian Ilan Pappé in *The Ethnic Cleansing of Palestine* writes:

> It is clear that by accepting the Partition Resolution, the UN totally ignored the ethnic composition of the country's population. Had the UN decided to make the territory the Jews had settled on in Palestine correspond with the size of their future state, they would have entitled them to no more than ten per cent of the land. But the UN accepted the nationalist claims the Zionist movement was making for Palestine and, furthermore, sought to compensate the Jews for the Nazi Holocaust in Europe.
> As a result, the Zionist movement was "given" a state that stretched over more than half of the country.[12]

Fifty-six percent of the land was given to a minority settler population. The partition plan was a historic crime that directly contributed to the savage war that Israel was to unleash on the Palestinian population. Pappé writes:

> But the moment the die was cast and people learned that the UN had voted overwhelmingly in favour of partitioning Palestine, law and order collapsed and a sense of foreboding descended of the final showdown that partition spelled. The chaos that followed produced the first Arab-Israeli war: the ethnic cleansing of the Palestinians had started.[13]

The first time the UN flexed its muscles, it greenlit a brewing genocide.

Australia and the Labor Party played a terrible role in this process. The Australian delegation to the UN in 1947, led by future Labor leader

---

12. Pappé 2007, p.51.
13. Pappé 2007, p.53.

HV "Doc" Evatt, pushed to establish UNSCOP. Evatt even chaired the committee. In recognition of this dubious service, he became the chair of the UN General Assembly in 1948. Australia's Labor government was the first to vote both in favour of partition and to recognise Israel.

The Nakba

There is no space here to recount in detail the horrors and destruction of Palestinian life Israel unleashed during the Nakba (catastrophe, in Arabic) of 1948. Over one million Palestinians were ethnically cleansed. Three-quarters of the refugees became a diaspora across the Middle East, the rest became refugees within Israel. Over 500 villages were destroyed by Zionist militias. After the Nakba, Israel claimed 78 percent of historic Palestine.

None of this was a surprise to the United Nations. Future Israeli Prime Minister David Ben-Gurion made no secret of the expansionist plans of Zionism. In 1947, the Zionist negotiators with the UN produced a map which incorporated all the land Israel would occupy during the Nakba. Ben-Gurion stated that the borders of Israel "'will be determined by force and not by the partition resolution".[14]

The partition plan, despite obvious intentions to ignore it, was beneficial to the Zionists. International recognition of the right to form a Jewish state in historic Palestine was immensely useful for the Zionist leadership. The UN gave diplomatic cover for their plans to ethnically cleanse Palestine.

Further, the UN was to oversee the process of partition after the British Mandate ended on 15 May 1948. The UN oversaw the expulsion of Palestinians. In Resolution 181, the UN said it would "prevent any attempt by either side to confiscate land that belonged to citizens of the other state, or the other national group".[15] UN forces took no such action. Initially, British Mandate authorities frustrated UN attempts to intervene, but after the British left the UN abandoned the Palestinians to their fate. UN forces merely watched and reported as Israel ethnically cleansed Palestine. To the degree UN forces intervened it was in favour

---

14. Quoted in Pappé 2007, p.56.
15. As paraphrased in Pappé 2007, p.126. For the full text of the resolution, see United Nations 1947.

of Israel. The first UN peacekeeping mission was launched during the 1948 Arab-Israeli war in an attempt to help enforce the partition of Palestine. By 1949, the peacekeeping mission assisted the "Armistice Agreements" that Israel signed with the defeated Arab armies, which codified Israeli control over land taken during the Nakba.

In 1949, the General Assembly admitted Israel as a full member state while denying the same right to Palestine. In the aftermath, the UN shed some crocodile tears but reaffirmed a two-state solution – the same "solution" which provided a framework for Israel's genocidal campaign in 1948. The United Nation Relief and Work Agency (UNRWA) was established in 1950. This new body was created to avoid the involvement of the International Refugee Organisation (IRO). Pappé writes:

> The IRO was the very same body that was assisting the Jewish refugees in Europe following the Second World War, and the Zionist organisations were keen to prevent anyone from making any possible association or even comparison between the two cases.[16]

UNRWA was established on the basis of not affirming the right of return for Palestinian refugees.

The role of UN forces after the Nakba followed a similar pattern of inaction that ultimately served Israel and its imperialist backers like America. Following the Israeli invasion of Egypt in 1956, UN forces were stationed in the Sinai Peninsula to act as a deterrent to further aggression. These forces were withdrawn just before the 1967 war, allowing Israel to occupy the peninsula.

UN forces stood idly by during the 1978 Israeli invasion of Lebanon. In just a few months in 1979, Israel led 148 attacks within UN-overseen areas. UN forces simply observed and documented.[17] In 1982, UN forces dissipated as Israel occupied Beirut and encouraged the fascistic Falange to butcher hundreds at the Sabra and Shatila Palestinian refugee camps.

---

16. Pappé 2007, pp.250–51.
17. Khalidi 1986, p.195.

The Oslo Accords

From Resolution 181 in 1947 to today, the United Nations has been unwaveringly committed to the so-called "two-state solution". In reality, this "solution" is a smokescreen for Israel's never-ending war on the Palestinians. As a demand, it is both hopelessly utopian and fundamentally unjust. Israel is an aggressive colonial state that is both expansionist and hostile to Palestinian self-determination. Israel will not let a genuine Palestinian state exist alongside it and has frustrated any possibility of one emerging. Yet the two-state solution is the framework from which the UN will not budge, the pattern set with the General Assembly's capitulation to Western imperialism and Zionism during partition. It is particularly jarring to see this framework still bandied about in UN resolutions as Israel seeks to smash any basis for the existence of a Palestinian state and civil society. The two-state solution ignores the plight of Palestinians within the Israeli state facing apartheid and systemic discrimination – an important fact missed by the much-lauded ICJ ruling and recent General Assembly motion symbolically demanding that Israel leave the Occupied Territories.

The height of the two-state farce was the Oslo Accords. On 13 September 1993 Israeli Prime Minister Yitzhak Rabin and Palestinian leader Yasser Arafat signed the Oslo Accords, the culmination of a "peace process" overseen by the US and the UN. The Oslo process had nothing to do with "peace" or with Palestinian rights. Israel had no interest in peace. The Accords were just the implementation of a modified Allon Plan, an Israeli plan to permanently incorporate the conquests of the 1967 Arab-Israeli War into Israel. It was the codification of more Israeli theft of historic Palestine:

> The United Nations partition plan said to the Palestinians you are going to have 47 of the 100 per cent that was originally yours. The 1993 Oslo agreement said to the Palestinians: you are going to have 22 of the 100 per cent that was originally yours.[18]

In return, the Palestinians were to receive a form of limited autonomy

---

18. Quoted in Anderson 2015.

and self-governance, but not sovereignty. In essence, a Bantustan system. The Palestine Liberation Organisation (PLO) under Arafat's leadership was allowed to set up the Palestinian Authority (PA) and became Israel's subcontracted prison guards of the Palestinian masses. Oslo II in 1995 even retained 60 percent of the West Bank under Israeli control. As Perry Anderson writes:

> The Palestinian Authority established in 1994, presented as a milestone in the struggle for national liberation, was in design a co-production of the West and of Israel, whose primary function was not to embody but to contain resistance to Zionism.[19]

Israel did not hold up its meagre end of the bargain. Post-Oslo Israel has accelerated its seizing of land in the West Bank. In the 31 years since Oslo the settler population in the West Bank has increased by 332 percent. The fastest increase in settlements occurred between 1993, immediately after the Accords were signed, and 2000.[20] Israel has only tightened the noose it has tied around the throat of Gaza since Oslo.

In return, Arafat and the PLO gave up nearly everything. Edward Said aptly described Oslo as "an instrument of Palestinian surrender, a Palestinian Versailles".[21] In a historic betrayal of the Palestinian national movement, Arafat renounced the claim of the Palestinian people to 80 percent of historic Palestine and accepted Israel's right to a Jewish state within the 1967 borders. Negotiations over the other major demands of the Palestinians – from the status of Jerusalem to the right of return – were relegated to a later stage.

The other legacy of the Oslo "peace process" is the idea that Israel is a reasonable actor committed to peace and that the Palestinian organisations outside the pliant Fatah, the dominant faction in the PLO, are the threat to peace.

Once again, under the banner of "peace" the UN had facilitated a historic defeat and injustice for the Palestinians.

---

19. Anderson 2015.
20. *Peace Now* 2023.
21. Said 1993.

What of the UN umbrella organisations?

The United Nations is more than just its peacekeeping forces. The UN runs and oversees a number of umbrella organisations and programs that claim a humanitarian purpose, such as the UNHCR (The Office of the United Nations High Commissioner for Refugees), UNICEF (United Nations Children's Fund) and UNESCO (United Nations Educational, Scientific, and Cultural Organization). These agencies reinforce the illusions many hold in the United Nations. Criticisms of Israel or other imperialist powers by various bodies and agencies of the UN are often held up as steps in the direction of justice.

There are several problems with this idea. A focus on the seemingly more harmless UN agencies misses the point that many UN-overseen organisations are outright terrible. Institutions such as the International Monetary Fund (IMF) and the World Trade Organization (WTO) are noxious imperialist bodies enforcing austerity and "structural adjustment" plans that keep Third World countries in cyclical debt crises. They do so in the service of the most powerful economies and their multinationals. The IMF and the WTO answer first and foremost to their most powerful participants, chiefly the US.

Sometimes the UN and its constituent organisations criticise the actions of Western governments. Human rights lawyers, academics and the like are often posted to particular humanitarian positions, like Francesca P Albanese, the United Nations Special Rapporteur on the Occupied Palestinian Territories. Albanese, in the face of a smear campaign by Israel and its supporters, has consistently told the truth about Israel's crimes against the Palestinians. In a speech to the National Press Club, she rightly criticised the Australian government's "amnesia", "myopia" and hypocrisy in its response to Israel's assault on Gaza.[22] The UN refused to sanction the American-led invasion of Iraq in 2003 and declared the invasion "illegal" in the face of US pressure for the UN to endorse the invasion. On the other hand, in the 1990s, the UN was the instrument through which the Clinton and Bush administrations enforced brutal US-led sanctions on Iraq.

However statements against particular actions taken by major

---

22. Manfield 2023.

imperialist powers do not equate to the UN being a force that could compel states to act otherwise. In the case of Iraq, America simply organised a "coalition of the willing" to support its invasion. The invasion went ahead at the cost of hundreds of thousands of Iraqi lives. Francesca Albanese said of the UN's response to Israel's genocide in Gaza: "The UN [is] experiencing its most epic political and humanitarian failure since its creation".[23]

Such statements are not just impotent anti-imperialist gestures. The UN seeks to manage the outcomes of imperialism, not oppose imperialism itself. In this sense, it is similar to the way bourgeois states attempt to manage the instability produced by capitalism domestically. Capitalism's anarchic nature creates a multitude of tensions and contradictions. Various state mechanisms are required to manage these and help stabilise the system, even when this can clash with the particular interests of sections of capital. For instance, the legal system can make judgments against huge companies to safeguard overall conditions of accumulation, such as the recent US anti-trust finding against Alphabet. This is not an anti-corporate action, but a measure to manage capitalism in the interests of capitalism.

As Leon Trotsky noted:

> Capitalism has transferred into the field of international relations the same methods applied by it in "regulating" the internal economic life of the nations. The path of competition is the path of systematically annihilating the small and medium-sized enterprises and of achieving the supremacy of big capital. World competition of the capitalist forces means the systematic subjection of the small, medium-sized and backward nations by the great and greatest capitalist powers.[24]

UN opposition to particular imperialist actions or denunciations of war crimes operate in the same way. It serves to smooth out the fraying edges of the world capitalist system in an attempt to stabilise it. Stabilisation is not anti-imperialist, it simply reinforces imperialism

---

23. Manfield 2023.
24. Trotsky 1944.

rather than challenging it. Managing imperialist excess is in no way equivalent to opposing imperialism itself.

Similarly, peacekeeping missions that seek to restore "order" serve the interests of the capitalist system. Without revolution, order can only mean capitalist order. Stability is a conservative principle. It accepts the existing world order and guarantees it to those who benefit from it. In the power games of geopolitics, the UN's stabilising role can only ever ultimately serve the interests of the most powerful states, not act as a neutral upholder of human rights. The rhetoric of UN humanitarianism obscures the reality of how intervention only exacerbates the problems of wherever the UN does intervene, while also legitimising imperialist meddling in poor countries.

UN in the West Bank post-Oslo

Even more purportedly benign UN bodies do not play a clearly positive role. Post-Oslo the UN and many of its umbrella institutions have become deeply enmeshed in the neoliberal functioning, or dysfunctioning, of the West Bank. UN agencies have been active in creating the situation in the West Bank, where a thin layer of Palestinian capitalists, along with the PA, have enriched themselves at the expense of the Palestinian masses.

This process is documented in Toufic Haddad's book *PALESTINE LTD: Neoliberalism and Nationalism in the Occupied Territory*. During the nineties, the UN embraced the neoliberal model of "development" and "nation building". In 1992, UN Secretary-General Boutros-Ghali talked of the shift beyond peacekeeping and into "questions of economic self-sufficiency". This model assumed that incremental economic development would bring about peace and lessen the risk of future conflict. Economic growth driven by the private sector was to be the cure-all. The UN resolved to work more cooperatively with its economic agencies like the WTO. Boutros-Ghali's successor as UN Secretary-General Kofi Annan stated:

> A fundamental shift has occurred in the UN-business relationship... The UN has developed a profound appreciation for the role of the private sector, its expertise, its motivated spirit,

its unparalleled ability to create jobs and wealth... In a world of common challenges and common vulnerabilities, the UN and business are finding common ground.[25]

It was, however, snake oil sold as a miracle cure. Post-Oslo development in the West Bank and the role of international aid is conditioned by what is acceptable to Israel. Haddad writes:

> Instead of placing in Palestinian hands the tools of their own development, under conditions in which they could exercise these powers, the international community and Israel placed select powers and resources in select hands, and under select conditions that were intended to reap political and institutional results.[26]

The political and institutional result was that economic "development" was used to reinforce the continued subordination of the Occupied Territories to Israel. The Israeli state still controls most aspects of Palestinian development and uses this to stifle serious independent economic development. Israel's expansionism in the West Bank reveals a commitment to de-developing Palestine.

A matrix of Western, UN and private-sector donor funding further controls the purse strings of the West Bank. Claiming a technocratic economic neutrality, such funding occurs on the basis of accepting Palestinian subordination. This is not a surprise considering much of the funding comes from Israel's Western allies. UN institutions simply give structure to this process. This is no small "contribution". Haddad notes that in 2012 the UN had 22 active bodies in the Occupied Territories and 412 projects listed as "underway" or "planned".[27] Little has changed over the past decade. Academic Anne Le More said of this process: "the US decides, the World Bank leads, the EU pays, the UN feeds".[28]

---

25. Quoted in Haddad 2016, p.29.
26. Haddad 2016, pp.116–17.
27. Haddad 2016, p.9.
28. Quoted in Haddad 2016, p.10.

Even if funding came from elsewhere, the neoliberal model of development means nothing much would change. Israel's subjugation of the Palestinians is primarily political and military, and no amount of economic development could change that. Palestinian decision-making is forced to exist within this narrow framework.

Haddad names this system "Palestine Ltd." He writes:

> Palestine Ltd. becomes neoliberalism's Janus-faced version of the former Palestine, emptied of any emancipatory liberationist content, and replaced with the economic and political strictures which enforce and deepen the state of oppression and fragmentation which Palestinians sought to overcome in the first place through their national liberation movement.[29]

Even aid services that can be a vital lifeline for Palestinians, like UNRWA, do precisely nothing to challenge the siege or Israeli state power. UNRWA, despite the ludicrous claims of the Israeli government, cannot be part of a political challenge to the Israeli state lest it lose funding from its major donors like the US, or is stopped from providing aid, as Israel is currently attempting to do. Repeated attacks on UNRWA and international aid bodies during Israel's campaign in Gaza do not change this logic.

This is a general problem with the international aid that the UN engages in. For it to be effective for its stated purpose of immediate relief, aid provision must not challenge the governments and institutions often responsible for humanitarian crises, lest the aid be blocked. UN international aid often acts to lessen the pressures on states to provide basic services and entrench the power of imperialists and foreign actors to control the affairs of small countries.

Can the UN be reformed?

The UN and similar international institutions are unreformable. Hypothetical plans for reform ignore the vital point that under capitalism, no international body like the United Nations can be formed

---

29. Haddad 2016, p.8.

against the interests of major imperialist powers. No other formation could be constructed that would not be a product of imperialism in every sense. Who would set up such a body, and how would it have any power?

Many argue that the central problem of the UN is the power of veto. However, calls to reform veto power or the size of the Security Council can often just reflect the growing ambitions of regional and sub-imperialist powers. For instance, Türkiye under Erdoğan has become a critic of the power of veto and make-up of the Security Council. In *A Fairer World is Possible*, Erdoğan opines:

> [The UN] has evolved into an institution that looks out for the interests of powerful nations instead of the entire world... Think of Palestine, which has been a bleeding wound for so many years. Can there be room for a mindset in the global conscience that aims to deprive the people of their native lands?[30]

Beyond the glaring hypocrisy of his denial of the rights of the Kurds to their native lands, Erdoğan's real wish is for his somewhat powerful nation to become even more so. Similarly, the G4 countries (Brazil, Germany, India and Japan) propose themselves to become permanent members of the Security Council. There is nothing intrinsically progressive about proposals to rejig the makeup of the Security Council and veto power.

Nor is the problem with the United Nations just the influence of the West. The world is dominated by imperialism, but imperialism does not impose one order. Imperialism is governed by power rivalries between multiple ruling classes, each as self-serving and murderous as each other. This competition is refracted through the UN.

China is one of five states with veto power. In 2017 China used this power, alongside Russia, to defend the Assad government from investigation over the use of chemical weapons against the Syrian revolution. In 1972, even when China was not a major imperialist power, it vetoed a resolution to admit the newly independent Bangladesh to the UN.

---

30. Erdoğan 2021, p.54.

The Maoist policy of "peaceful co-existence" meant accommodation to neighbouring countries like Pakistan, no matter the crimes they committed against their own people.

Today, most of the UN peacekeeping forces are from formerly colonised countries. UN forces in Lebanon are primarily from Indonesia, India, Ghana, and Nepal.[31] Currently, hundreds of Kenyan police are stationed in Haiti as part of yet another UN intervention into the country. The Kenyan police have long been a force of violent oppression against the people of Kenya. Just this year the police killed scores of protesters during the #RejectFinanceBill movement. The withdrawal of Kenyan police from Haiti was a demand of the movement.

In the UN General Assembly, the leaders of postcolonial and smaller nations sometimes utter denunciations of the crimes of the imperialist powers. Beyond their powerlessness, such speeches are more geared towards domestic consumption. Often they are just the political theatre of rulers desperate for some positive PR. In a recent session of the Assembly, Jordan's King Abdullah II condemned Israel's actions in Gaza as "unprecedented atrocities"[32] that cannot be justified. He failed to mention Jordan's long history of collaboration with Israel.

Even if the great powers at the top of the Security Council could be replaced, the records of smaller nations inspire no hope. Multilateral institutions of local groups of ruling classes have proved just as terrible and useless as the United Nations. The role of the Arab League is emblematic of this. The Arab League remains steadfastly inactive in the face of Israel's destruction of Gaza. An "extraordinary gathering" of the Arab League and the Organisation for Islamic Cooperation in November decided to do nothing. They might as well not have met. Almost a third of League members have already, or have been in the process of normalising ties with Israel. Assad, the butcher of the Syrian revolution, was readmitted to the League last year.

The Arab ruling classes, or any ruling class for that matter, oppress and exploit the people within their own borders – how can they be expected to stand up for justice in Palestine or elsewhere?

---

31. United Nations Peacekeeping 2024.
32. *All Arab News* 2024.

The ICJ and the ICC

South Africa's application to the International Court of Justice (ICJ) charging Israel with genocide in Gaza was greeted with hope and praise by the majority of Palestine supporters and the left. It is often argued that the court's finding, that Palestinians had "plausible rights to protection from genocide" at the hands of Israel, opens up more space for the Palestine movement. Both the exhaustive presentation of the scale and barbarity of Israel's crimes and the ICJ ruling are pointed to as serious ideological blows to Israel and its backers.

There is a grain of truth to this, but the impact of the ruling is almost always overstated. While it is the case that the hallowed halls of the Hague refusing to let Israel off the hook has ideological value, this is not the first occasion an ICJ ruling has gone against Israel. In 2004, the ICJ published an advisory opinion that the construction of Israel's apartheid wall dividing the West Bank was illegal and "tantamount to de facto annexation".[33] Like the 2023 ruling, this was described as a moral victory. But it had little to no impact on broader Palestine sentiment, despite the legal defeat for Israel.

The latest ICJ ruling has been quickly forgotten for the most part. At best, the ruling confirmed and somewhat extended the mass sentiment that has been expressed and driven forward by the Palestine movement. At the same time, the ICJ acted in a manner to take just enough of a stance to maintain its legitimacy.

The 2004 ruling did not stop the construction of the border wall, nor did the 2023 ruling stop Israel's genocide. On the day of the ICJ interim ruling, Israel reportedly killed 174 people in Gaza. There was no call for a ceasefire, despite the ICJ ruling that the Israeli state must take "immediate and effective measures" to prevent genocidal acts. The court did not make a ruling on South Africa's first request for the ICJ to instruct Israel to "immediately suspend its military operation in and against Gaza". How is this seriously different from the line taken by the United States, Australia and other supporters of Israel, of hollow rhetoric without any actions to make Israel stop? The fact that Israel would have ignored the order is little excuse. As the Gazan journalist

---

33. International Court of Justice 2004.

Bisan Owda said, the ICJ "forgot to demand a ceasefire".[34] She posted on Instagram: "The ICJ is a lie!! There is no justice in the World!!" The ruling was another example of the toothless "humanitarianism" of UN institutions and international law.

The ICJ has a long history of ignoring the crimes of the US and other major powers. Right after its founding in 1946, the ICJ declined to test the legality of the UN partition plan for Palestine. The demands of Palestinian representatives and the Arab delegations were ignored. American violations of international law are very rarely brought before the ICJ. The US's crimes in Vietnam, Iraq, Afghanistan and so on have never been brought to the Hague.

When the court does criticise the major imperialist powers, the latter just ignore it. The ICJ found that the US support for the Contras against the Sandinista regime and mining of Nicaragua's harbours was illegal in 1986. The decision was dismissed by the US government, which refused to recognise ICJ jurisdiction. Two Security Council motions about the decisions were vetoed by the US. The ICJ has no ability to independently enforce its positions. This is by design. The ICJ, created as the UN's judicial arm, mirrors the problems with the UN itself. The ability to enforce decisions against major imperialist states would have made it a worthless tool for the imperialist interests that dominated it, and the broader UN's creation.

The ICJ, like the UN, exists on the basis of imperialism and its hierarchies. There can be no supra-imperialist body that can sit above geopolitics and adjudicate. The impotence of the ICJ in the face of Israel and its imperialist backers reflects this. It is not a flaw in the ICJ, but rather the body working as intended – issuing legal rulings which can be used to discipline smaller nations via the Security Council yet will never discipline powerful nations.

International law plays an important ideological role for imperialism too. ICJ rulings bolster the illusion that the destructive anarchy of the world system could be rationalised and serve human rights. Legality under international law is often mistaken for morality. As China Miéville notes:

---

34. Bisan Owda, Instagram, 27 January 2024.

> There is a danger that basing "progressive" critique on international law might, to a jurist's potential horror, precisely legitimate those actions for which powerful states are able to garner overwhelming or authoritative legal support.[35]

When states marshal international law behind their imperialist designs, the socialist approach to a conflict should not change. Any war must be judged on its class and political content, not whether a majority of international legal opinion thinks it is justified. Legality is not a barometer of political content.

The same is true of the International Criminal Court (ICC) and its chief prosecutor's application for arrest warrants against Israeli Prime Minister Netanyahu and Defence Minister Yoav Gallant for alleged war crimes. Hamas leaders were also named in the application despite the massive and incomparable difference between the crimes of Israel and the actions of Hamas. The false equivalence is jarring. Further, the application remains caught in legal limbo, with the arrest warrants yet to be issued. Even if they are, what state could force Israel or its allies to arrest Netanyahu?

The ICC itself was a product of years of international discussion and negotiation organised through the United Nations. It followed a similar pattern of empty rhetoric and hypocritical toothlessness against the major powers. Ad hoc tribunals established by the Security Council in the early 1990s in response to genocides in Bosnia and Rwanda gave impetus to a push to set up a permanent court, resulting in the 1998 Rome Statute. The ICC was founded four years later.

America played a central role in negotiations, attempting to make sure it was not subject to ICC jurisdiction. This failed initially. The Rome Statute allowed the court to prosecute members of non-signatory states, therefore including the US. In response, the US voted against the Rome Statute in 1998. The other six countries that voted against the treaty included Israel and China. Israel objected to the inclusion of "transferring population into occupied territory" as a war crime.[36]

US President Bill Clinton signed onto the Rome Statute on his way

---

35. Miéville 2005, p.298.
36. United Nations 1998.

out of office in 2000 but it was all for show. He refused to submit his decision to the Senate for ratification. Under George Bush, America refused to join the ICC or to ratify the Rome Statute. The US concluded over a hundred agreements with different countries removing US military personnel from such risk. America even passed The Hague Invasion Act, giving itself the right to authorise military force to "liberate" any American or citizen of a US-allied country being held by the ICC. The US also warned participants in the ICC that they risked losing all US military assistance unless they pledged to protect Americans serving in their countries from any ICC prosecutions. Perry Anderson notes:

> Naturally enough, the ICC – staffed by pliable personnel – declined to investigate any US or European actions whatever in Iraq or Afghanistan, concentrating its zeal entirely on countries in Africa, according to the unspoken maxim: one law for the rich, another for the poor.[37]

The history of the ICC is a demonstration of the ability of the US to bend institutions of international law to its will. Even if multilateral deals, like the Rome statute, or particular court decisions are annoyances to the US, they mean little. They are "annoyances" in the same way a fly annoys a bull but means little to it.

Conclusion

Israel's impunity to commit genocide and war crimes, with ironclad support from the West, breeds a temptation to search for glimmers of hope in UN resolutions and ICJ rulings. Surely these forces could do something? A deep source of the illusions in such forces is a sense of powerlessness in the face of Israeli barbarism that continues to escalate.

In the struggle for Palestine and against imperialism, it is vital to be rid of illusions. Appeals to the United Nations and international law are counterproductive. Both are barriers in the anti-imperialist struggle, not even fair-weather friends. Both serve imperialism rather

---

37. Anderson 2023.

than challenge it. The UN and bodies like the ICJ cannot be part of a strategy for Palestinian liberation – you cannot use a fork to eat soup. Reliance on international law often just deflects attention from mass action and towards institutions like the ICJ, the ICC and the UN that are dominated by the imperialist aims of the US and its allies.

The core of imperialism is not international bodies and diplomacy, but the hard power of economic and military might. It is this that has to be challenged and ultimately defeated. Arguments to look to the UN are coloured by a deep pessimism about the potential of working-class struggle. Yet it is precisely this force, the working class, which holds the power to challenge imperialism and capitalism.

The fact that working-class struggle is at a low ebb does not mean we should lower our political horizons and standards. Rosa Luxemburg wrote of how the laws and pacts of capitalist diplomacy can not only never bring peace, but are an obstacle to anti-war struggle:

> The bourgeois friends of peace are endeavouring – and from their point of view this is perfectly logical and explicable – to invent all sorts of "practical" projects for gradually restraining militarism, are naturally inclined…to take every expression of the ruling diplomacy in this vein at its word. … [Socialists, however,] must consider it their duty…to expose the bourgeois attempts to restrain militarism as pitiful half measures, …and to oppose the bourgeois claims and pretences with the ruthless analysis of capitalist reality.[38]

The temptation to look to various bourgeois actors to substitute for class struggle and mass movements needs to be resisted.

References

All Arab News 2024, "Jordan's King delivers blistering condemnation of Israel at UN, meets with new Iranian President", 24 September. https://allarab.news/jordans-king-delivers-blistering-condemnation-of-israel-at-un-meets-with-new-iranian-president/

---

38. Luxemburg 1980, p.251.

Anderson, Perry 2015, "The House of Zion", *New Left Review*, 96, November/December. https://newleftreview.org/issues/ii96/articles/perry-anderson-the-house-of-zion

Anderson, Perry 2023, "The Standard of Civilization", *New Left Review*, 143, September/October. https://newleftreview.org/issues/ii143/articles/perry-anderson-the-standard-of-civilization

Baxter, John 1999, "Is the UN an alternative to 'humanitarian imperialism'?", *International Socialism*, 2:85, Winter. https://www.marxists.org/history/etol/newspape/isj2/1999/isj2-085/baxter.htm

Erdoğan, Recep Tayyip 2021, *A Fairer World is Possible*, Turkuvaz Kitap.

Haddad, Toufic 2016, *PALESTINE LTD: Neoliberalism and Nationalism in the Occupied Territory*, I.B. Tauris.

International Committee of the Red Cross 1949, *Geneva Convention Relative to the Protection of Civilian Persons in the Time of War*, Geneva, pp.153–221.

International Court of Justice 2004, *Legal Consequences of the Construction of a Wall in the Occupied Palestinian Territory*. https://www.icj-cij.org/case/131

Khalidi, Rashid 1986, *Under Siege: PLO Decision making during the 1982 War*, Columbia University Press.

Kolko, Gabriel 1990, *The Politics of War: The World and United States Policy 1943–1945*, Random House.

Lenin, VI 1966 [1920], "Speech Delivered At A Conference Of Chairmen Of Uyezd, Volost And Village Executive Committees Of Moscow Gubernia", 15 October, *Collected Works*, 31, Progress Publishers. https://www.marxists.org/archive/lenin/works/1920/oct/15b.htm

Luxemburg, Rosa 1980 [1911], "Peace Utopias", *Rosa Luxemburg Speaks*, Pathfinder Press. https://www.marxists.org/archive/luxemburg/1911/05/11.htm

Manfield, Evelyn 2023, "Top UN expert on occupied Palestinian territories takes aim at global response to war", *ABC News*, 14 November. https://www.abc.net.au/news/2023-11-14/francesca-albanese-un-palestinian-territories-press-club/103103448

Marx, Karl 1887, *Capital*, Volume 1 (Chapter 10, Section 1). https://www.marxists.org/archive/marx/works/1867-c1/ch10.htm

Miéville, China 2005, *Between Equal Rights: A Marxist Theory of International Law*, Haymarket Books.

Pappé, Ilan 2007, *The Ethnic Cleansing of Palestine*, Oneworld Publications.

Peace Now (Settlement Watch) 2023, "30 Years After Oslo – The data that shows how the settlements proliferated following the Oslo Accords", September. https://peacenow.org.il/en/30-years-after-oslo-the-data-that-shows-how-the-settlements-proliferated-following-the-oslo-accords

Rees, Stuart 2023, "What happened to the UN's 'Responsibility to Protect'?", *Pearls and Irritations*, 24 November. https://johnmenadue.com/what-happened-to-the-uns-responsibility-to-protect/

Said, Edward 1993, "The Morning After", *London Review of Books*, 15 (20), 21 October. https://www.lrb.co.uk/the-paper/v15/n20/edward-said/the-morning-after

Trotsky, Leon 1944 [1915–16], "The Program of Peace", *Fourth International*, 5 (9). https://www.marxists.org/history/etol/newspape/fi/vol05/no09/trotsky.htm

United Nations 1945, United Nations Charter. https://www.un.org/en/about-us/un-charter/full-text

United Nations 1947, *Palestine Plan of Partition with Economic Union – General Assembly Resolution 181 (II)*. https://www.un.org/unispal/document/auto-insert-185393/

United Nations 1998, Press Release L/2889, "UN diplomatic conference concludes in Rome with decision to establish permanent international criminal court", 20 July. https://press.un.org/en/1998/19980720.l2889.html

United Nations Peacekeeping 2024, "UNIFIL Factsheet", April.

Vanzler Joseph 1945, *"The United Nations" – A New Thieves' Kitchen*, *Fourth International*, 6 (8), August. https://www.marxists.org/history/etol/writers/wright/1945/08/uno.htm

NICK EVERETT

Labor's long embrace with apartheid Israel

Nick Everett is a long-term socialist activist and chair of Friends of Palestine Western Australia.

WHEN ISRAEL LAUNCHED its genocidal war on Gaza last October, Australian Foreign Minister Penny Wong was quick to pick Israel's side. "We stand with Israel and we always will", Wong told the Australia-Israel Chamber of Commerce. Wong equated the State of Israel's resolve to wage war on the Palestinians with the "resilience and courage [of Jewish people] in the face of thousands of years of persecution and many of the worst atrocities in human history".[1]

Wong boasted of the role played by "Australia's most consequential foreign minister, Doc Evatt", who "was a leading architect of the partition plan that laid the foundations for the creation of a new nation state". Just as Evatt backed the partition of Palestine in 1947, Wong insisted that a new (or not so new) partition plan – the "two-state solution", in which Palestinians are given "statehood" in a mere morsel of their homeland – is needed to bring peace between Israelis and Palestinians. That the two-state solution has never eventuated has, according to Wong, nothing to do with Israel's determination to maintain its 57-year-long occupation of Gaza, the West Bank and East Jerusalem through settlement expansion and a brutal siege of Gaza.

---

1. Wong 2023.

Instead, it's the actions of Hamas that have "pushed that two-state solution further out of reach", she asserted.[2]

Labor's rhetoric has shifted somewhat over the past year. With the International Court of Justice arguing that Israel's occupation of the Palestinian territories is illegal and that there is a plausible case Israel is committing a genocide against the Palestinians, the Albanese government has felt compelled to tone down its enthusiasm for Israel's actions. However, it has steadfastly opposed implementing sanctions against the apartheid state. To date, Australian sanctions target just seven individual Israeli settlers, despite their violent attacks on West Bank Palestinians being actively encouraged by Israeli government ministers.

When former West Australian Labor Senator Fatima Payman put the case for wide-ranging sanctions against Israel, she faced scorn from across Labor's front bench, leading to her resignation from the Labor parliamentary caucus. Labor senators joined with the opposition to condemn as "antisemitic" the slogan "From the river to the sea, Palestine will be free", which Payman had used to end her 15 May media statement.[3] Seeking to reinforce the argument that Palestine supporters are violent antisemites, Labor member for Wills Peter Khalil accused protesters outside his office of "violence, intimidation, harassment, hate speech and damage of property".[4] Prime Minister Anthony Albanese has since appointed Khalil to the role of Special Envoy for Social Cohesion and arch-Zionist Jillian Segal AO[5] to the role of Special Envoy to Combat Antisemitism.

So why is Labor so pro-Israel?

A number of arguments have been advanced to explain Labor's stance. One is that the Zionist lobby exercises an all-powerful influence within the corridors of federal parliament, to the extent that it can dictate Labor party policy. Another is that because Australia shares with Israel a common history of settler colonialism, successive

---

2. Wong 2023.
3. Knott 2024.
4. Karp 2024.
5. Albanese 2024. Segal is the former President of the Executive Council of Australian Jewry and Chair of the Australia-Israel Chamber of Commerce.

Australian governments are compelled to back Israel's dispossession of the Palestinians. This article will address those arguments before presenting an alternative thesis. I will argue that Australia's relationship with Israel is an extension of the US alliance, which has been a cornerstone of Australian foreign policy since the beginning of the Cold War. Israel's relationship to US imperial power can be likened to Australia's "deputy sheriff" role in the South Pacific. Neither nation is simply a "lap dog" for US imperialism. Both nations' ruling classes share a common interest in having the protection of a mightier imperial power while advancing their own interests in the region.

Following World War II, with the British Empire in rapid decline, the Chifley Labor government began to pursue a foreign policy more independent of Britain than that advocated by the conservative opposition leader, Robert Menzies. Both recognised the Middle East's significance for global shipping and trade. However, whereas Australian conservatives looked to Britain and its client Arab regimes as key allies in the Middle East, Chifley and Evatt saw in the creation of Israel a potential new ally at the outset of the Cold War.

In the interwar years, Labor Zionism (or "Socialist Zionism") had come to dominate the politics of Jewish settlers in Palestine. Labor Zionists employed socialist rhetoric to draw labour movement support behind their nationalist, colonial-settler project. In doing so, they galvanised support from both European social democratic parties and the labour parties in Britain and Australia. Thus, Labor could more readily sell the *idea of Israel* to its base than could Menzies' Liberal Party. Before moving on to discuss Labor Zionism, this article will look at the Zionist lobby's influence on Australian foreign policy and Australia and Israel's shared history of settler colonialism.

An "all powerful" Zionist lobby?

Several former Labour politicians, such as Bob Carr, Kevin Rudd and Paul Keating, have argued that the Zionist lobby exercises such a powerful influence in the media that it can bring down governments too critical of Israel. Former foreign minister Bob Carr argues that the Zionist lobby is able to dictate Australia's foreign policy to the detriment of Australia's "national interest".[6] However, the "national interests" that Labor holds dear are not the interests of the Australian working class but the interests of big business. And Australian big business today overwhelmingly favours a close relationship with Washington as a protector of its interests in the Asia Pacific. It should therefore be no surprise that Israel – Washington's most important ally in the Middle East – gains favourable media coverage and red-carpet treatment from Australian politicians.

Albanese and Wong both hail from the Labor Left. Albanese was a founding member of the Parliamentary Friends of Palestine and early in his parliamentary career spoke inside and outside parliament in opposition to Israel's occupation of Palestine. However, his conversion to backing Israel follows in a long Labor tradition in which the US alliance is viewed as sacred. This conversion can't simply be explained by him having been seduced by Zionist lobbyists.

Foreign policy is not and has never been shaped primarily by sectionalist lobby groups. While many nation states and interest groups lobby the Australian government, the positions the government adopts can't be explained simply or primarily by them being at the bidding of a well-resourced team of lobbyists in Canberra. Australian foreign policy serves the collective, geopolitical interests of the Australian ruling class. To understand how support for Israel has become so central to Australian foreign policy, we need to examine the historical circumstances that have given rise to the Australia-Israel relationship, who benefits from it and how.

Settler colonialism

Australia shares with Israel settler-colonial origins. However, whereas the Australian nation state began as a federation of colonial outposts of the British Empire, Zionism's claim to Israel was asserted on an entirely different basis. Zionists have always insisted they are not colonisers but rather derive their claim from a biblical connection with the Holy Land. With Israel having gained statehood at a time when the Great Powers were having to concede independence to powerful anti-colonial

---

6. Carr 2022.

movements, it was untenable for mid-twentieth century Zionists to admit to being colonisers. However, they *are* colonisers and have never shied away from employing racism to advance their aims.

In his 1896 pamphlet, *The State of Jews*, the father of modern Zionism Theodor Herzl pursued the support of European colonial powers with his claim that a Jewish state in Palestine would form "a portion of the rampart of Europe against Asia, an outpost of civilisation against barbarism".[7] Similarly, last July Israeli Prime Minister Benjamin Netanyahu told the US Congress that the current genocide in Gaza is "a clash between barbarism and civilisation, between those who glorify death and those who sanctify life".[8]

While Zionists' violent usurpation of Palestinian land is an ongoing contemporary project, the question of who controls the land in Australia was resolved long ago in the British colonisers' favour. A century-long frontier war across the entire continent ended when British soldiers crushed the last surviving Aboriginal resistance in the Kimberley region of Western Australia in the 1890s.

Britain's imperial conquest reduced Australia's Indigenous population to a tiny minority. Disease, loss of land and direct violence reduced the Aboriginal population by an estimated 90 percent by 1900. By the time of Federation, Aboriginal people numbered just 3 percent of Australia's total population, and their numbers have never recovered. From the early twentieth century onwards, when it became apparent that Aboriginal people were not simply going to "die out", Australian states and the Commonwealth government set about seeking to absorb surviving First Nations people into White Australia through a policy of assimilation; child removal (the Stolen Generations) was a key strategy. In contrast, Zionism has always sought to exclude indigenous Palestinians from residence and full citizenship rights in the State of Israel.

Israel is not, and has never been, simply an outpost of a grand imperial power. Though British Lord Balfour declared the Empire's support for a Jewish state in Palestine in 1917, the Balfour Declaration fell short of the demands of Zionist leaders. It did not go as far as

---

7. Herzl 1988, p.85.
8. Cited in Moor 2024.

declaring support for an *exclusively* Jewish state, stipulating that "nothing shall be done which may prejudice the civil and religious rights of existing non-Jewish communities in Palestine".[9]

Balfour was hardly a man of his word. Indeed, various promises were made to Arab leaders and allied powers that were seemingly contradictory. The Balfour Declaration, which formed part of Britain's colonial mandate in Palestine, formalised by the League of Nations in 1922, sought to balance the interests of Zionist settlers against those of Arabs. Prior to the Declaration, Sir Henry McMahon, the British high commissioner in Egypt, wrote to Sharif Hussein bin Ali, Emir of Mecca, promising British support for an independent Arab state in exchange for Arab assistance in opposing the Ottoman Empire. Simultaneously, Britain undertook secret negotiations with France to dismember the Ottoman Empire and divide Syria, Iraq, Lebanon and Palestine between them, culminating in the Sykes Picot agreement, signed in 1916.

With British colonisers simultaneously seeking to curry favour with both Zionist settlers and Arab elites, the Zionist movement could little afford to be simply an appendage to British imperial designs. To succeed, Zionists needed to steer their own course, appealing to the Jewish diaspora in Europe to cultivate a new sense of nationhood based on a conquest of both Palestinian land and economy.

A Jewish nation?
The central founding myth of Zionism was the idea that the Jewish diaspora constituted a nation. Herzl argued that antisemitism was inherent in non-Jews, leaving Jews with no choice but to emigrate from Europe and establish a new Jewish homeland. Simultaneously, a radical tradition was developing among Yiddish-speaking workers in the Russian empire, who formed the Jewish Labour Bund in 1897. For these socialist Jews, the solution to combatting antisemitism was not emigration, but instead fighting for rights and autonomy within the tsarist empire through strikes, protest and working-class agitation.

The coming of World War I brought various competing nationalisms to the fore. Russian revolutionary Vladimir Lenin synthesised an

---

9. *Balfour Declaration 1917* [n.d.].

analysis of modern imperialism, which he described as "the highest stage of capitalism", to explain how competing European powers were driven towards "an annexationist, predatory, plunderous war...a war for the division of the world, for the partition and repartition of colonies, 'spheres of influence' of finance capital, etc." [10]

Lenin's pamphlet served as a denunciation of the opportunist leaders of the Second International who had backed the belligerent nations in the war. It also served to develop further Lenin's view that oppressed nations – those subjugated by imperialism – should have the right to self-determination. A 1913 pamphlet by Joseph Stalin, *Marxism and the National Question*, articulated what constituted a nation: "a historically constituted, stable community of people, formed on the basis of a common language, territory, economic life, and psychological make-up manifested in a common culture". [11]

The Bolsheviks argued that the Jewish diaspora did not constitute a nation as they lacked a common language or territory. Stalin polemicised against the much looser definition of a nation put forward by the Austrian socialist Otto Bauer: "a nation is an aggregate of people bound into a community of character by a common destiny".[12] Such a definition, according to Stalin, conceded ground to nationalism, of which Zionism was just one example. Zionism, he explained, is "a reactionary nationalist trend of the Jewish bourgeoisie...[that] endeavoured to isolate the Jewish working-class masses from the general struggle of the proletariat".[13]

There was nothing antisemitic in the argument that Jews were not a nation. Jews constituted an important part of the working classes (often the most militant element), as well as of the bourgeoisie and petty bourgeoisie, across central and eastern Europe. Antisemitism had arisen in a specific historical juncture as competing nationalisms sought to define Russian, Polish, Hungarian and other identities as distinct from Jewish culture and religion. In contrast to Zionism,

---

10. Lenin 1920.
11. Stalin 1913. Stalin's views on the national question were strongly influenced by fellow Bolsheviks Nikolai Bukharin and Vladimir Lenin.
12. Stalin 1913.
13. Stalin 1913.

Bolshevism argued that the solution to Jewish oppression lay in the overthrow of capitalism and recognition of cultural autonomy of Jews within a federation of socialist republics.

However, within the Jewish Bund, a separate and distinct ideological current emerged that attempted to reconcile socialism with Jewish nationalism. As the revolutionary wave that engulfed Europe at the end of World War I receded, this Zionist current gained ground. Though Zionism remained a minority view among European Jewry, "socialist" Zionism dominated among the Russian and Polish Jews who migrated to Palestine after the defeat of the 1905 Revolution. Between 1904 and 1914, 35,000–45,000 Jews arrived in Palestine from Russia and Poland, collectively known as the Second *Aliyah* (migration). It should be emphasised, however, that the Zionist Jews who migrated to Palestine in this period were a tiny minority of the mass migration of Eastern European Jews. According to Zachary Lockman, of the approximately 2.4 million Jews who left eastern Europe between 1881 and the First World War, 85 percent went to the United States and just 3 percent migrated to Palestine.[14]

Labor Zionism

Labor Zionism emerged as a political current in 1905, with the formation of Poale Zion (Workers of Zion). Poale Zion soon began to forge relationships with the social democratic parties organised within the Second International. Its emerging right faction, which openly espoused nationalism, had much in common ideologically with the social democratic and labour parties that lined up behind their own ruling classes during World War I. As we shall see, Labor Zionism's growing hegemony within the settler Jewish population of Palestine in the interwar years contributed to the Australian Labor Party's subsequent support for Israel's creation following World War II.

Poale Zion's most prominent intellectual was Dov Ber Borokhov, a self-described Marxist. Borokhov argued for Jewish colonisation of Palestine on the basis that the Jewish proletariat could take power through a common class struggle with the Arab proletariat. However,

---

14. Lockman 1996, p.17.

Borokhov had no doubt as to the supposed cultural and economic superiority of Jews:

> It is the Jewish immigrants who will undertake the development of the forces of production of Eretz Yisra'el [Palestine], and the local population of Eretz Yisra'el [the Arabs] will soon assimilate economically and culturally to the Jews.[15]

Poale Zion's followers, mostly eastern European middle-class urban Jews, saw it their task to transform themselves into agricultural or industrial wage workers, thus creating a Jewish proletariat in Palestine that could advance the class struggle within Palestine's developing capitalist economy. Another left-Zionist party, Hapo'el Hatza'ir ("The Young Worker"), influenced by Tolstoyan principles and rejecting Marxism and class struggle, sought to build a new society through physical labour, self-sacrifice and settlement on the land. Both used the term "conquest of labour" to describe the construction of Jewish proletariat in Palestine through the embrace of hard physical labour, especially in agriculture.[16]

However, this schema soon collided with a contrasting reality on the ground. Neither Jewish nor non-Jewish capital rushed to invest in Palestine, an overwhelmingly rural economy. Nor were there bountiful jobs for newly arrived Jewish settlers. Farmers, especially citrus plantation owners, preferred Arab labour, which they considered cheaper, more experienced and more reliable. With Arab wages too low for subsistence for newly arrived Jewish settlers, many idealistic Jews returned home. For those who remained, the "conquest of labour" soon came to take on a new meaning: the creation of a Jewish labour market through the exclusion of Arab labour. This policy went hand-in hand with the "conquest of the land" (establishing Jewish ownership of as much of the land as possible, whether through purchase or expropriation) and "produce of the land" (boycotting Arab-made goods to grow a market for Jewish agriculture and industry).[17]

---

15. Borokhov, "Our Platform", 1906. Cited in Lockman 1996, p.25.
16. Lockman, 1996, p.28. See also Glazer 2007.
17. Lockman 1976, p.5.

Following World War I, Poale Zion split into left and right factions over the question of participation in bourgeois-led Zionist institutions. The nationalist, right faction formed Ahdut Ha'avoda (United Labor) under the leadership of future Israeli prime minister David Ben-Gurion, who had emigrated to Palestine in 1906. Whereas the First *Aliyah* had established settlements on a capitalist basis, with subordinate Arab labour, Ben-Gurion and his followers argued that cooperatives should be established that excluded Arab labour. This new policy, he argued, would have better prospects of success. Ben-Gurion emerged as a master of employing socialist rhetoric, while having an eye for a strategy that could enlist bourgeois Zionist support.

In 1920, 4,500 Jewish workers from the parties Ahdut Ha'avoda and Hapo'el Hatza'ir elected delegates to a labour congress, which formed Histadrut, the General Federation of Hebrew Workers in Eretz Israel. Ben-Gurion was elected Histadrut's first secretary-general. A decade later, Ahdut Ha'avoda and Hapo'el Hatza'ir merged to form Mifleget Poalei Eretz Yisrael (Workers Party of the Land of Israel, known by the acronym MAPAI), with Ben-Gurion the party's secretary.

Both parties envisaged the Histadrut not as a trade union federation in the classic sense, but rather as an instrument to facilitate the colonisation of Palestine by Jewish workers and the establishment of a Jewish state. As its name suggests, the Histadrut was to be a union of Jewish workers only; Arab workers were to be excluded. The Histadrut was an instrument for state building and the class struggle could take a back seat. As historian Mitchel Cohen observes, Ben-Gurion "acted forcefully to centralize the Histadrut's resources and power structure as a nascent workers' state within the state of Mandate Palestine".[18]

The Histadrut built a whole array of institutions for this purpose, including a disability fund (Kupat Cholim), labour exchanges, building firms (Solel Boneh), a company for the sale of agricultural products (Tnuva), a wholesale cooperative (Hamashbir Hamerkazi), a labour schools' network, housing and agricultural cooperatives (*kibbutzim*), and even a bank. "The bank is the true expression of the workers' will",

---

18. Cohen 1992, p.109.

declared Yosef Aharonowitz, co-director of the bank and a central leader of Hapo'el Hatza'ir, in 1922.[19]

The Histadrut attempted to enact what it termed "constructive socialism". In reality, this meant subordinating supposedly socialist goals to the nationalist goals of Zionism. A workers' society (Hevrat ha-Ovdim), a collective holding company through which Histadrut enterprises operated, supposedly gave every Jewish worker in Palestine a stake in the workers' economy. However, Hevrat ha-Ovdim's secretary-general, Reiner, made clear what the institution's real priorities were, stating: "We believe in socialist ownership but a capitalistic way of management; moreover, profit is not a 'dirty word' with us; it is a phrase which guides our general economic thinking".[20]

Expressing his condescension towards the working class, Reiner stated:

> Frankly, [workers] are laymen; they do not grasp the wider implications of running a business; they can't read a balance sheet; they are weak on long range planning; these workers have a dozen other weaknesses as members of the Board of Directors [of Histadrut-affiliated firms]. But they contribute mightily in another field: they understand management's viewpoint much better and they pass this message on in one form or another, generally without even thinking about it, to their fellow workers. Secondly, management sees the workers' viewpoint much, much better, and like the workers, we absorb this viewpoint without even concentrating on it. The result? Strikes in our enterprises are few and far between. Labor and management exist in much greater harmony.[21]

Demonstrating Labor Zionism's ability to subordinate and control Jewish workers, while excluding Arabs from Jewish economic life, proved key to its ascendency and decades-long hegemony within the Zionist movement. The Histadrut could exercise an iron discipline over

---

19. Sternhell 1998, p.38.
20. Reiner, cited in Lockman 1976, p.7.
21. Reiner, cited in Lockman 1976, p.7.

its membership because so many members owed their employment to the Histadrut, whose enterprises were financed by Zionist capitalists abroad. Indeed, up until the 1980s, the Histadrut commanded the Israeli economy as union, boss and healthcare provider for the majority of Jewish workers in Israel.

Moreover, the Histadrut experienced spectacular growth, drawing large numbers of Jewish workers into its ranks and extolling the virtues of its project to entice other European Jewish workers to make *Aliyah* (migrate to Palestine). According to its executive committee, the Histadrut numbered 8,394 members in 1923, 22,538 in 1927, 35,389 by the beginning of 1933, and more than 100,000 by the outbreak of World War II. Its membership grew dramatically during and after World War II, with a new influx of Jewish migrants. At the end of 1949, eighteen months after Israel's declaration of independence, the Histadrut numbered more than 250,000 and, a year later, 330,000 (46 percent of the adult Jewish population).[22]

However, the massive growth of the ranks of the Histadrut during and after World War II had less to do with the pull factor of Jews being drawn to Labor Zionist ideology and more to do with the push factor of the devastating Nazi Holocaust in Europe. In contrast with the preceding waves of Jewish migration, European Jews now arrived in Palestine not because they were committed to the Zionist cause, but because they had nowhere else to go. Between 1925 and 1965, the United States sharply limited Eastern European migration via a quota system, closing its doors to large numbers of would-be Jewish immigrants. Similar immigration restrictions operated in Canada, Britain, Australia and South Africa, all of which favoured non-Jewish European immigration.[23]

In 1933, soon after coming to power in Germany, the Nazi regime reached the Haavara agreement with the Labor Zionist leadership in Palestine, facilitating the Nazi takeover of Jewish property. Under this agreement, 60,000 German Jews were allowed to migrate to Palestine between 1933 and 1939. For those Jews who survived the Nazi Holocaust and arrived in the displaced persons camps, many would no doubt have

22. Sternhell 1998, pp.179–80.
23. Karpf 2002.

preferred to migrate to the United States or other Western countries, but found Palestine their only option. In 1948 alone, more than 120,000 Jewish immigrants arrived in Palestine.[24]

The Histadrut buttressed its economic power with military force from its inception. In 1920, the year of its foundation, the Histadrut established a militia known as the Haganah, later a key instrument for the ethnic cleansing of Palestine and the precursor to the Israeli Defence Forces. By the time of Israel's 1948 declaration of independence, the Haganah numbered 20,000.[25] It was a well-trained paramilitary force, having collaborated with the British to suppress the Palestinian revolt between 1936 and 1939, and after World War II was well placed to lead the insurgency against the British.

During the British Mandate period, Labor Zionism achieved unrivalled authority in the Yishuv (Jewish Palestine). In 1935, Ben-Gurion, leader of both the Histadrut and MAPAI, was elected chair of the Jewish Agency executive, the Yishuv political leadership. While MAPAI never attained a majority within the decision-making bodies of the Zionist Organisation (the umbrella organisation of the Zionist movement), or later in Israel's parliament, it exercised effective political control of the Yishuv during the British Mandate period and led a succession of Israeli coalition governments until it merged into the Israeli Labor Party in 1968. The Labor Party remained dominant in Israeli politics for a further decade, until the coalition it led ceded power to the right-wing Likud party in 1977, ending three decades of Labor Zionist rule.

The evolution of Labor Zionism outlined above bears both similarities to and differences from other social democratic and labour parties. In the lead-up to World War I, European social democratic parties accommodated to capitalism and threw their support behind their own ruling classes in the carnage that followed. They advocated a parliamentary road to socialism, whereby the winning of reforms would ultimately legislate socialism into existence. Where they were able to shepherd once combative labour movements behind them, and

---

24. For a discussion of the forces that drove Jews to Palestine in this period see Segev 2019, chapter 14.
25. Sternhell 1998, p.392.

bring about stable conditions for capitalist investment, they became increasingly entrusted by the bourgeoisie with the task of government.

Labor Zionism similarly subordinated its supposedly socialist goals to the immediate tasks of nation building, though its consolidation as a hegemonic ideological current in Palestine predates the formation of the state of Israel by some decades. In Australia at the turn of the twentieth century, Labor parties in each state cohered around a national platform of support for the White Australia policy, arbitration of industrial disputes and defence of Empire. Racial exclusion bound together Labor's first federal caucus in 1901, which was otherwise divided between opposing camps of protectionists and free traders.

In Australia, it was non-white migrant labour, rather than Indigenous labour, that was the target of the White Australia Policy. However, Australian Labor leaders used similar justifications to their Labor Zionist comrades: to maintain high wages, cheap labour had to be excluded, they argued, and class peace enforced via a highly regulated labour market. In fact, Ben-Gurion and other Histadrut leaders gave more *rhetorical* support to the idea of organising Arab labour in Palestine than did Australian Workers Union leaders to organising Chinese labour in Australia. However, in reality, this rhetoric was employed as a means to deflect criticism by left Zionists and internationalists. During the period of the British Mandate, numerous opportunities for a united struggle between Jewish and Arab workers were studiously avoided and even undermined by Histadrut leaders.[26]

Zionism and the international left

Whereas other nationalist movements that arose in the late nineteenth and early twentieth centuries sought to expel colonising powers, Zionism was itself from the outset a colonising movement, albeit one that claimed to be a national liberation movement. It could only succeed in creating an exclusively Jewish state in Palestine via the dispossession, expulsion and oppression of the Palestinian people. As Lockman has observed, the left in the Yishuv (and later in Israel) faced a dilemma:

---

26. For a series of case studies, see Lockman 1996.

Those parties which adhered to Zionism (whatever their particular brand of "synthesis" between Zionism and Marxism) were compelled, by the logic of their very presence and goals in Palestine, to compromise their socialist principles one by one when they came into conflict with the demands of Zionist colonization; but those parties which refused any compromise with Zionism found themselves relatively isolated, cut off from the great majority of the Jews of the Yishuv, and later the state, and this of course severely limited the possibilities of playing a prominent role in the class struggle.[27]

From its inception in 1919, the Communist International (Comintern) took a strong stance against Zionism, reflecting the Bolsheviks' opposition to all forms of nationalism outlined previously. The Comintern and its affiliate, the Palestinian Communist Party (PCP), strongly backed the 1929 Arab massacres of Jewish civilians in Hebron. In 1936, when the Palestinian revolt erupted, the PCP gave it full support, giving uncritical backing to the leadership of al-Hajj Amin al-Husayni.[28]

In the lead-up to and during World War II, Comintern policy under Stalin's leadership followed a series of zig-zags driven by the Soviet Union's foreign policy. From 1928, the Comintern adopted the ultraleft "Third Period" line, branding Labor and social democratic parties as "social fascist". From the mid-1930s, under the "popular front" policy, working-class interests were to be subordinated to the needs of "progressive" capitalists who opposed fascism. After Stalin signed a peace treaty with Hitler in August 1939, a new line emerged. The Comintern denounced the "inter-imperialist war" until June 1941, when Hitler launched a major military offensive against the Soviet Union. Stalin then directed another U-turn: the "inter-imperialist war" now became a "people's war" to defeat fascism. In 1943, the Comintern itself was dissolved as an act of appeasement to the Soviet Union's World War II allies.

These zig-zags had a profoundly disorienting impact on rank-and-file communists worldwide. Over the course of the 1930s,

---
27. Lockman 1976, p.3.
28. For further detail on the PCP's history during this period, see Budeiri 2010.

revolutionaries who didn't accept the line dictated by Stalin and his lieutenants found themselves marginalised or expelled from Comintern-affiliated communist parties. New party leaderships loyal to Moscow were installed and internal democracy was extinguished. However, it was undoubtedly a bitter pill to swallow for many communists when, in May 1947, the Soviet Union announced that it would support the UN plan for partitioning Palestine and creating a Jewish state.

The Soviet Union's UN ambassador, Andrei Gromyko, told the United Nations General Assembly that Moscow favoured a bi-national state in Palestine, but that:

> [if] such a solution proves unworkable because of the deteriorated relations between the Jews and the Arabs, it will be necessary to examine a second solution…namely, the partition of the country into two independent autonomous states, a Jewish one and an Arab one.[29]

Five months later, the Soviet Union and its Eastern European satellite states voted in favour of UN Resolution 181, which called for Palestine's partition and subsequently supported Israel's May 1948 declaration of independence. According to historian Philip Mendes, Moscow's support for Israel included:

> vigorous diplomatic support whereby the Soviet Union defended Israel's right to self-defence in United Nations debates, and condemned the "armed aggression" directed against the Jewish state. They also defended Israel's right to retain strategically significant territory such as the Negev region captured in the war, and rejected any Israeli responsibility for the Palestinian refugee problem.[30]

The Soviet Union also channelled military supplies to Israel via Czechoslovakia and trained Haganah pilots and paratroopers. The

---

29. Cited in Mendes 2009, pp.138–39.
30. Mendes 2009, p.139.

military aid contributed to Israel's rapid defeat of the Arab armies that had entered Palestine, leading Ben-Gurion to later conclude: "[The Soviet Union] saved the country, I have no doubt of that. The Czech arms deal was the greatest help, it saved us and without it I very much doubt if we could have survived the first month".[31]

Communist parties around the world quickly fell into line, with the US Communist Party describing Israel as "an organic part of the world struggle for peace and democracy" based on a "struggle against British and Anglo-American imperialist domination".[32] The French Communist Party likened the Haganah's role in the Israel "war of independence" (in reality a campaign of ethnic cleansing) to the national liberation struggles and anti-fascist movements of the Chinese communists, the Viet Minh, the Greek partisans and the Spanish Republicans.[33]

Stalin's enthusiastic backing for the new Zionist state was based on the premise that Zionists, rather than Arabs, were more likely to succeed in hastening a British withdrawal from Palestine and weaken British imperialism's grip on the Middle East. With the Cold War in its infancy, Stalin may have also hoped, naively, that the USSR could counter Washington's growing influence in the Middle East by having the state of Israel on its side. That, however, was not to happen. The effect of Stalin's capitulation to Zionism was to isolate Arab communist parties and bolster Arab nationalism. Additionally, when Labor and European social democratic parties voiced support for Palestine's partition, they faced little left-wing dissent, either from inside or outside their ranks.

According to Mendes, the British Labour Party backed a Jewish state in Palestine as early as August 1917. British Labour parliamentarians had, in the preceding years, demonstrated their loyalty to King and Country by enthusiastically backing the British Empire's sacrifice of hundreds of thousands of men on the blood-soaked battlefields of France and Belgium. Later, in 1944, a British Labour Party conference resolved that Jews should be admitted to Palestine "in such numbers as

---

31. Kramer 2017, p.7.
32. Mendes 2009, p.139.
33. Mendes 2009, p.139.

to become a majority" and that "the Arabs be encouraged to move out [to neighbouring countries] as the Jews move in".[34]

In the years 1945–48, the Attlee Labour government did not implement this position, reflecting the British ruling class's animosity to a terror campaign directed at British troops in Palestine by Zionist militias that they considered a threat to ongoing British influence in the Middle East. However, the aspirations of Zionists to a Jewish homeland in Palestine continued to influence the ranks of the British Labour Party and other Western social democratic parties. The impact of the Nazi Holocaust, and its destruction of the Jewish labour movement in Europe, only served to accelerate this sentiment.

Zionism and the Australian left

In the aftermath of World War II, there was virtually universal support for Israel's creation among the Australian left, spearheaded by the Communist Party of Australia (CPA) and the Jewish Council to Combat Fascism and Anti-Semitism. Mendes cites two examples of CPA and union leaders expressing support for Zionist goals as early as 1945. In February that year, communist and Federated Iron Workers general secretary Ernie Thornton supported a resolution of the World Trade Union Congress in London calling for a Jewish homeland in Palestine.[35] Six months later, Victorian CPA leader Ralph Gibson expressed support for Jews to enter "their historical homeland" and establish their "national home" in the CPA's Victorian newspaper, *The Voice*.[36]

In 1947, the CPA welcomed the United Nations partition plan for Palestine and, a year later, backed Israel's declaration of statehood. Gibson led the campaign to rally CPA support behind Israel, authoring a pamphlet that equated Zionism's efforts to conquer Palestine with anti-imperialist struggles in China, Vietnam and Greece.[37] Gibson argued the war between Israel and Arab military forces was a "war on the Jews…being waged by 'kings' from outside the country" in concert with British imperialism. By suppressing Zionist terror attacks

---

34. Mendes 2009, p.137.
35. Thornton 1945.
36. Gibson 1945.
37. Gibson 1948.

and imprisoning Zionist leaders, argued Gibson, the British occupation forces in Palestine had "fanned the anti-Jewish feeling of Arab reactionaries and strengthened the influence of the reactionary Jewish terrorist gangs".[38]

The CPA loyally followed directions from Moscow: Labor Zionists were supposedly a progressive force seeking to liberate Palestine from British colonial rule and unite Jewish and Arab workers around a common program, while the reactionary Irgun and Stern Gang[39] were seeking to stoke the flames of sectarian division. However, it was the Labor Zionists, led by Ben-Gurion and constituting the leadership of the Jewish Agency in Palestine, who bore prime responsibility for the 1948 Palestinian *Nakba* (catastrophe), a campaign of ethnic cleansing that drove large numbers of Palestinians into a permanent exile from their homeland. It was their militia, the Haganah, affiliated with the Histadrut and armed and trained by Britain in the preceding decade, that was most central to the Zionists' terror campaign.

The CPA's newspaper *Tribune* presented the state of Israel as the underdog, backed by the Soviet Union and confronting a more powerful enemy in the form of Arab regimes supported by British and American oil interests. In March 1948, two months before Israel's declaration of statehood, *Tribune* published a letter by ten prominent left-wing Australians defending the UN partition plan, which they claimed, "shows a proper understanding of the sufferings which the Jewish people have undergone", and condemned "pro-fascist Arab leaders" who opposed it.[40]

Subsequent *Tribune* articles condemned what the paper claimed was an "Arab invasion of Palestine" made possible "with British and American planes and arms" and urged the Chifley government to maintain its support for Palestine's partition.[41] *Tribune* asserted that Jews in Palestine were "being sacrificed by both British and US imperialists for the sake of enormous oil profits which they hope to garner in

---

38. Gibson 1948.
39. The Irgun and Stern Gang were far-right Zionist groups which conducted terrorist activities against both the British Mandate administration and Palestinians.
40. Blackburn et al 1948.
41. "Imperialists hamstrung United Nations move for Palestine peace", *Tribune*, 19 May 1948, p.1.

alliance with Arab chieftains" and claimed that "atrocities by Jewish extremists are being featured in the British press, to the exclusion of similar Arab atrocities".[42]

Other prominent leftists also backed Israel. Journalist Wilfred Burchett equated the Jewish struggle for independence in Palestine with that of the Spanish Republicans confronting a common fascist enemy.[43] Feminist Jessie Street was another strong supporter of a Jewish "national homeland" in Palestine.[44] Labor politicians, including NSW premier William McKell, Marrickville MP Carlo Lazzarini and Bondi MP Abram (Abe) Landa, as well as ACTU president (and later Bendigo MP) Percy James Clarey, were also prominent supporters of Israel.[45]

The Jewish Council to Combat Fascism and Anti-Semitism

The Melbourne-based Jewish Council to Combat Fascism and Anti-Semitism was significant in shaping left-wing opinion. The Council, established in 1942, was a coalition of Jewish social democrats, communists and liberals, including figures such as Norman Rothfield, Sam Goldbloom, Judah Waten and Sam Cohen.[46] The Victorian Jewish Board of Deputies (VJBD) and the Executive Council of Australian Jewry (ECAJ), the peak Victorian and national bodies of Australian Jewry, delegated the Council with undertaking public relations and political lobbying activities on their behalf.[47] In the years following World War II, the Council's influence overshadowed that of the Jewish Bund in Melbourne, which had been the political home for anti-Zionist Eastern European Jews who had migrated to Australia in the interwar years.[48]

The Council began to advocate for a Jewish state in Palestine from May 1945. Three years later, it campaigned for recognition and support for Israel, working with Zionist organisations, Jewish cultural organisations and the CPA-aligned Jewish Progressive Centre to

---

42. "Oil is key to Palestine sellout", *Tribune*, 14 April 1948, p.2.
43. Burchett 2007, pp.17–19.
44. Rutland 1990.
45. Mendes 2009, p.142.
46. Mendes 2009, p.143.
47. Mendes 2009, p.143.
48. For more on the Bund in Melbourne, see Slucki 2018.

organise pro-Israel public meetings, rallies, radio broadcasts and news articles.[49] The Council also widely distributed two pamphlets by Evelyn Rothfield, the Council's information officer and president of the Women's International League for Peace and Freedom (WILPF).[50] In *Whither Palestine* (1947), Rothfield defends Jewish mass migration to Palestine (in opposition to then British policy) and asserts that the Arab-Jewish conflict was due to the malign influence of exploitative Arab landowners and the Mufti of Jerusalem, whom she branded a Nazi collaborator.[51] In *Israel Reborn* (1948), Rothfield claims that only Arab feudal landlords opposed partition. In a similar vein to contemporaneous articles in *Tribune*, Rothfield asserts that "the large mass of Arabs inside Palestine have little quarrel with their Jewish neighbours".[52]

A May 1948 Council petition calling for immediate Australian recognition of Israel gained the support of leading ALP figures Jim Cairns (Snr), William Slater, Doris Blackburn and Frank Crean, as well as Communist trade union leaders Clarrie O'Shea and Jim Healy. According to Mendes, the Council distributed 55,000 copies of a pamphlet based on this petition. The CPA also actively promoted and distributed the Council's literature.[53]

The CPA and its fellow travellers on the left remained silent about the Palestinians' own desire for liberation from colonial rule and their mass displacement by Zionist colonisers. Writing in 2004, former CPA member Max Watts recalls how the CPA turned its back on the plight of the Palestinians:

> The Palestinians? They had been, early on, totally defeated, were now being expelled or were leaving. We lefties, to our shame, almost ignored their plight. For us, the Left, the invading Arab

---

49. Mendes 2009, p.144.
50. Evelyn Rothfield remained active in WILPF and the peace movement for another four decades. In 1984 Evelyn and her husband Norman Rothfield were founding members of the Australian Jewish Democratic Society (AJDS). They both advocated for the Palestine Liberation Organization's recognition of the State of Israel and were strongly supportive of the Oslo Accords. See chapter 8: "Women, peace and security" in Laing 2023.
51. Rothfield 1947.
52. Rothfield 1948.
53. Mendes 2009, p.144.

armies, even the Palestinian fighters, were but British puppets, colonial troops, fighting to maintain endangered parts of the failing empire.[54]

Labor and the birth of Israel

The Australian Labor Party endorsed Israel's creation as early as 1943, when its national conference resolved to support "the continued growth of the Jewish national home in Palestine by immigration and settlement".[55] This position was generally reflective of the views within the Australian left at the time, as outlined above. However, it did not align with the policy of the Curtin Labor government.

Between 1936 and 1939, the conservative Lyons government strongly backed Britain's violent suppression of the Palestinian Revolt with no protest from the Labor opposition. During World War II, both Lyon's successor, Robert Menzies, and Labor Prime Minister John Curtin continued to back British colonial rule in Palestine. Each shared Britain's fear of an Arab backlash against the declaration of a Jewish state. It was not until 1947 that Curtin's successor Ben Chifley and his external affairs minister Herbert "Doc" Evatt began to chart a different course, advocating for the creation of a Jewish state in Palestine.

Evatt was instrumental to the United Nations General Assembly vote in favour of Palestine's partition. Firstly, he led the Australian UN delegation, which in May 1947 successfully moved to establish the UN Committee on Palestine (UNSCOP). On 31 August 1947 UNSCOP released its report: it unanimously supported an end to the British mandate, while a majority of the committee recommended the partition of Palestine between Arab and Jewish states.

Secondly, Evatt chaired the Ad Hoc Committee on the Palestinian Question, appointed by the UN General Assembly to provide it with recommendations. A majority of this committee similarly recommended Palestine's partition, proposing to the UN General Assembly that 56 percent of Mandate Palestine be allocated to a Jewish state, even though Jewish settlers numbered less than one-third of Palestine's

---

54. Watts 2004, pp.108–9.
55. Weller and Lloyd 1978, p.267.

population. Jerusalem was proposed to be an international zone, excluded from the territory of both states.

On 29 November 1947 the UN General Assembly adopted UNSCOP's partition plan, with 33 member nations voting in favour (including Australia), 13 voting against and 10 abstaining (including the United Kingdom). The vote marked a rare break with British foreign policy at the time. Evatt's role in advocating for the UN partition plan led historian Chanan Reich to describe Evatt as "one of the godfathers of the present Israeli state".[56]

At midnight on 14 May 1948 Ben-Gurion, as head of the Jewish Agency in Palestine, proclaimed the establishment of the State of Israel. US President Harry Truman recognised the provisional Zionist government as the *de facto* authority in Israel just eleven minutes after Ben-Gurion's proclamation. The Soviet Union was the first state to give *de jure* recognition to Israel, doing so three days later. However, the Chifley Labor government waited until 27 January 1949 to formally recognise the State of Israel, doing so in concert with the British government.[57]

The proclamation came amidst a wave of Zionist terror. Between late 1947 and early 1949, 530 Palestinian villages were ethnically cleansed, 15,000 Palestinians were killed and 750,000 more were forced into exile. Three neighbouring Arab states – Egypt, Transjordan and Syria – invaded Palestinian territories allocated for a future Arab state, ostensibly to defend Palestinians from a Zionist takeover. However, Transjordan's King Abdullah I sent in troops, not to liberate Palestine, but to occupy the West Bank with the intention of annexing the territory. Poorly trained Egyptian and Syrian forces were soon overrun by the better trained Haganah, Palmach and Irgun. By the end of the war, in mid-1949, the new state of Israel controlled 78 percent of historic Palestine.

During the Arab-Israeli war, Evatt opposed a plan authored by the UN's special mediator for Palestine (the Bernadotte Plan), which attempted to pressure Israel to cede the Negev region. Following the

---

56. Reich 2002, p.36.
57. Harris 2012.

Australian government's recognition of Israel, Evatt lobbied strongly for Israel's admission to the UN, in May 1949.

Historians have put forward various arguments as to why the Chifley government strongly advocated for Israel. Rodney Gouttman claims that relations between Australia and Israel were not founded "because of strategic or economic necessity" but "on the personal beliefs of Dr Herbert Vere Evatt".[58] Philip Mendes argues that the Zionist movement's lobbying of Evatt was "very significant in confirming Evatt's pro-Israel sentiments".[59] He cites the support Evatt expressed for Israel's creation in a 1943 meeting with the Jewish Advisory Board of New South Wales and his close relationship with Zionists such as Max Freilich, president of the State Zionist Council of New South Wales, and Labor parliamentarian Abram Landa.[60] Mendes also observes that it was almost exclusively the conservative parties and the antisemitic far right who articulated anti-Zionist and pro-Arab views, often accusing Zionists of being associated with communism and seeking to undermine the British Empire.[61]

Evatt was no doubt influenced by the strong pro-Israel sentiments expressed by Labor Party allies and the wider left. Evatt himself cited "a feeling of deep compassion for the Jews" in the aftermath of their "merciless persecution by the Germans under Hitler" as key to his desire "for a speedy settlement of the Palestine question".[62] However, Evatt's own views and the influence of those around him don't explain the significant shift in foreign policy enacted by the Chifley government as a whole. Instead, we need to explore the wider context of post-World War II geopolitics.

Forging the US alliance on the eve of the Cold War

At the end of World War II, the United States emerged as the world's pre-eminent superpower, with the British Empire in terminal decline. The Middle East soon became a key battleground in the Cold War as the

---

58. Gouttman 1987, p.262.
59. Mendes 2009, p.146.
60. Mendes 2009, p.142.
61. Mendes 2009, p.145.
62. Evatt 1949, p.163.

US sought to isolate and defeat its rival, the Soviet Union. Both powers vied for allies to protect strategic trade routes through the Suez Canal. The Middle East was especially important to US imperialism because of its vast oil reserves. And Israel, which had just won a decisive military victory, was viewed favourably for its potential to help safeguard US interests.

As Israel's UN ambassador Danny Danon put it:

> From the moment President Truman became the first world leader to recognize the new Jewish state, Israel has had no better friend than the United States of America, and the U.S. has had no more steadfast ally than the state of Israel.[63]

In this new Cold War reality, Chifley began to reorient Australian foreign policy, shifting allegiance from a declining British Empire towards the United States. Of particular concern to the Australian ruling class was the growing strength of China under the rule of the Chinese Communist Party, which defeated its nationalist rivals, the Guomindang in October 1949. An alliance with the US was viewed as the best means to safeguard Australian interests in the Asia Pacific. In exchange, Australia would play the role of deputy lieutenant, aiding US global expansionism. The ANZUS treaty, signed in 1951 by the Menzies government, formalised the pact. However, it was Chifley who laid the foundation for the Cold War policies pursued by his successor Robert Menzies.

A damaging split within Labor, resulting in the formation of the anti-communist Democratic Labor Party, kept Labor out of government for the next two decades. During the 1956 Suez crisis, when Israel invaded the Sinai with British and French military support, Menzies defended Israel's actions, painting Egypt, whose territory had been invaded, as the villain. Evatt, Labor's opposition leader, opposed Menzies' trenchant support for British and French imperialism, declaring their Suez Canal invasion "a naked exercise of military power".[64] Evatt's position aligned with the US, the Soviet Union and the UN, who

---

63. Kramer 2007, p.1.
64. "Evatt says: 'it's illegal'", *The Argus*, 2 November 1956, p.4.

together pressured Israel, the United Kingdom and France to withdraw troops from Egypt. Evatt's stance foreshadowed that of the Whitlam government which espoused an "impartial" approach to conflict between Israel and its neighbours while arguing that Arab states should recognise Israel and make peace with the Zionist state.

Gough Whitlam succeeded Arthur Calwell as Labor opposition leader in February 1967. According to Zionist writers Colin Rubenstein and Tzvi Fleischer, "the opposition, under Gough Whitlam who had visited Israel in 1964 and again shortly after the war, was at least as pro-Israeli as the government".[65] Various Labor Party conferences passed resolutions urging Israel's recognition by Arab states and in August 1964, Whitlam accused the Menzies government of having succumbed to Arab pressure, stating in parliament that it had not done enough to improve post and air communications with Israel.[66]

The Whitlam Labor Government

When Labor returned to government in 1972, Israel had become the Middle East's most powerful military state and a key pillar of US hegemony in the region. While Israel's 1948 foundation faced no significant opposition within the Australian left, Israel's 1967 invasion of the remainder of historic Palestine (the West Bank, East Jerusalem and Gaza), as well as the Syrian Golan Heights, received a very different response. The 1967 Six Day War between Israel and Egypt, Syria and Jordan coincided with a massive escalation in the US war in Vietnam and the introduction of conscription in Australia. By 1968, a powerful anti-war movement had developed, and its impact was being felt within Labor's base as trade unionists became increasingly involved in anti-war protest. Labor's left faction began to express its solidarity with Palestinians.

At the beginning of his term, Whitlam made his pro-Israel stance clear, telling a Sydney Town Hall meeting:

> [While being neutral on the Middle East conflict] we are not neutral on the question of the sovereignty of Israel. The rights of

---

65. Rubenstein and Fleischer 2007.
66. Reich 2002, pp.125–28.

Jews to a national homeland and to live there in peace are not to be denied. The right of Israel to defend her borders and preserve intact the great democracy which flourishes there is not a matter on which any Australian Government has been neutral.[67]

The 1973 Yom Kippur War, however, proved to be a turning point. While the US backed Israel unconditionally, the Whitlam Labor government felt compelled to adopt a more cautious, independent approach. Australia did not condemn the Syrian and Egyptian attacks on Israel but did condemn US weapons being airlifted in to support Israel. While officially adopting a position of neutrality, Whitlam and most of his cabinet colleagues remained sympathetic to Israel.

In 1985, Whitlam wrote:

> Australian Governments had always professed an even-handed attitude towards Israel and the Arab nations in international forums, while in practice they were thought to be favouring Israel in the 1948, 1956 and 1967 conflicts. When the 1973 conflict erupted it was expected that my Government would favour Israel... On this occasion Australia had to practise its profession of even-handedness.[68]

Several factors influenced the Whitlam government's position. The end of the White Australia policy meant that Arab voters, though still a small minority, now emerged as a lobby in support of Palestinian rights. Whitlam was also focused on building a relationship with Indonesia's military regime, led by General Suharto, and newly independent Malaysia, both Muslim states. Additionally, Whitlam needed to retain support for his government from the party's left faction.

Whitlam's deputy Jim Cairns had been a prominent figure within the anti-Vietnam War movement. The elevation of Cairns and other prominent Victorian left party members into the cabinet was an attempt to co-opt anti-war and left-wing sentiment. Enlisting Cairns and other leading luminaries of the Labor left for Whitlam's business-friendly

---

67. Quoted in Harris 2012, p.12.
68. Whitlam 1985, pp.124–26.

agenda required making some concessions. This was reflected in a somewhat more critical stance towards US imperialism, both in the Middle East and in South East Asia.

In 1974, Australia's UN ambassador announced that "if the Palestinians want to create a state of their own alongside Israel, we will accept this",[69] committing Australia for the first time to supporting a two-state solution. Before his dismissal, in November 1975, Whitlam even approved establishing a Palestinian Liberation Organization (PLO) liaison office in Canberra.

However, this more progressive approach was not without its critics inside the ALP. One of the most vocal Labor supporters of Israel was Bob Hawke, elected Labor president in 1974. As ACTU president Hawke visited Israel on two occasions in the early 1970s, seeking close relations with both the Histadrut and the Israeli Labor Party, which had governed Israel since its inception. Hawke attacked Whitlam's stance on the Yom Kippur War and wrote a booklet arguing Israel's case.[70]

Hawke became Australia's next Labor prime minister in 1983, having had a cosy relationship with the US embassy in Canberra in the preceding Fraser years.[71] Once elected prime minister, Hawke embraced a neoliberal agenda and reasserted a close relationship with Washington. He also became the first Australian prime minister to visit Israel. At a press conference during his 1987 visit, Hawke rejected the idea of a Palestinian state in favour of Jordanian-Palestinian confederation (a position advocated also by the last Trump administration in 2018) and insisted that Israel couldn't be expected to negotiate with the PLO until "there is a clear recognition by the PLO of Israel's right to exist".[72]

In a speech in Sydney following his return, Hawke gushed praise for the Israeli state and its Labor Zionist founders:

> As a social democrat, I could not fail to respect the way in which Israel had incarnated the vision of David Ben-Gurion of a

---

69. Quoted in Harris 2012, p.13.
70. Rubinstein 1991, p.538.
71. Sparrow 2021.
72. Hawke 1987a.

working class building its own nation through its own physical and intellectual labour. What particularly impressed me, however, was the fundamental fact that Israel was a democracy, a remarkable democracy, incessantly engaged in democratic disputation about every aspect of national policy.[73]

Labor since the Oslo Accords

Perhaps more attuned to *realpolitik*, Hawke's successor Paul Keating threw his support behind the Oslo Accords and established Labor's long-standing support for a two-state solution. The Accords, adopted by Israeli Prime Minister Yitzhak Rabin and PLO leader Yasser Arafat at a ceremony on the White House lawns in September 1993, were heralded as laying the foundation for Palestinian self-rule in the Occupied Territories, and a pathway towards a Palestinian state.

However, they proved to be a *cul-de-sac* for the Palestinian liberation struggle. Palestinian writer Edward Said accurately described the Accords as "an instrument of Palestinian surrender, a Palestinian Versailles".[74] Arafat renounced the claim of the Palestinian people to 80 percent of historic Palestine and agreed to postpone negotiations regarding the final status of Jerusalem, the Occupied Territories, water, sovereignty, security, the illegal Israeli settlements and the right of return for Palestinian refugees to the last stage of the "peace process".[75]

Israel gave no guarantee regarding the right of the Palestinian people to self-determination, national independence and statehood. Israel did not renounce control over the Palestinian territories it had occupied since 1967, nor did it agree to withdraw troops or dismantle the settlements it had been building since the 1970s.

Since the Oslo Accords, settlements have nearly tripled. In 1993 there were approximately 110,000 Israeli settlers in 128 West Bank settlements and a further 140,000 settlers residing in East Jerusalem. Thirty years later, that number had soared to 465,000 settlers in 300 West Bank settlements and more than 230,000 settlers in East

---

73. Hawke 1987b.
74. Said 1993.
75. Bullimore 2023.

Jerusalem, according to Israeli NGO, Peace Now.[76] Last year, the Israeli state approved 30,000 new settlement housing units, a 180 percent increase over the past five years.[77] Settler violence has increased to unprecedented levels, encouraged by ministers within Netanyahu's far-right coalition government.

During the past three decades, Labor, along with other social democratic parties, has repeated the mantra of a "two state solution" *ad nauseum*, accompanied by the refrain "Israel has a right to defend itself". In 2009, these words were used by deputy Prime Minister Julia Gillard to defend Israel's bombing of the defenceless and blockaded civilian population of Gaza. Today, Albanese and Wong use the same words to defend Israel's genocide in Gaza and bombing of Lebanon.

Conclusion

Whether in opposition or in government, Labor has always been heavily committed to Israel. This policy began at the time of Israel's bloody creation, at the outset of the Cold War. Recognition of and support for Israel formed part of the Chifley Labor government's reorientation of Australian foreign policy away from its historic close relationship with Britain towards an alliance with US imperialism that continues to this day. That the Stalinist left at the time overwhelmingly supported Israel aided Chifley and Evatt in selling the idea of Israel to Labor's base.

To the extent that the Whitlam Labor government embarked on a foreign policy more independent of Washington and critical of Israel, it proved to be the exception rather than the rule. Since Oslo, Labor has used rhetorical support for a "two-state solution" to feign support for a peaceful Middle East. However, Labor's defence of Israel's repeated bombings and invasions of Gaza and Lebanon, asserting "Israel has a right to defend itself", as well as its support for the deployment of Australian troops in Iraq and Afghanistan, show this claim to be a farce.

The Albanese government – and Labor governments before it – could have done much more to pressure Israel to end its brutal siege of Gaza and the genocide of the past 12 months, as well as Israel's suffocating military occupation in the West Bank. Imposing diplomatic,

---

76. Peace Now 2023.
77. European Union 2024.

trade and military sanctions would have been a start. Instead, even implementing a national conference resolution committing Labor to recognise a Palestinian state at some point in the future has proven a step too far for the Albanese government, fearing that it would alienate Israel's far-right government.

Labor backs Israel not because it has a powerful Zionist lobby in its ear, or because its politicians are (mostly) descended from a long line of settler colonists, but because backing Israel forms part of Canberra's commitment to the US alliance. Since the end of World War II, the Australian ruling class has looked to the United States to protect its interests in the Asia Pacific in exchange for Australian government support, including military support, for US intervention abroad, especially in the Middle East and Southeast Asia.

Moreover, Labor's insistence on a "two-state solution" is and always has been a capitulation to Zionism. It is premised on the idea that Jews cannot live side by side with Muslim and Christian Palestinians within the same state. Such a "solution" – if it were ever to be implemented – would hold Palestinians hostage in a fragmented territory surrounded by walls and checkpoints, leaving Israeli apartheid intact.

Genuine liberation requires tearing down the state structures of oppression and racism that Zionism has created, structures now intertwined with Israeli and regional capitalism. It will require a revolutionary struggle by the Arab masses to overthrow their corrupt and capitalist regimes and establish socialist states throughout the Middle East.

Such a solution may seem utopian while bombs rain down on Lebanon, and Egyptians, Jordanians and Arabs across the region fear brutal repression for displays of Palestinian solidarity. However, the Arab regimes, many of which owe their existence to US military aid, are more fragile than they may appear, as the 2010–11 Arab Spring demonstrated. Here in Australia, we must remain focused on the task of building a mass Palestine solidarity movement that unequivocally demands freedom for Palestine, from the river to the sea.

References

Albanese, Anthony 2024, "Special envoy to combat Antisemitism", 9 July. https://www.pm.gov.au/media/special-envoy-combat-antisemitism

Balfour Declaration 1917 [n.d.], Yale Law School. https://avalon.law.yale.edu/20th_century/balfour.asp

Blackburn, Doris et al 1948, "Terrorism not main factor in Palestine", *Tribune*, 13 March, p.5.

Budeiri, Musa 2010 [1979], *The Palestine Communist Party, 1919–1948: Arab and Jew in the Struggle for Internationalism*, Haymarket Books.

Bullimore, Kim 2023, "The farce of Oslo 20 years on", *Red Flag*, 22 September. https://redflag.org.au/article/farce-oslo-20-years

Burchett, William 2007 [1944], chapter 3: "Who is Wingate anyway?" in Burchett, George, and Nick Shimmin (eds) 2007, *Rebel Journalism: The Writings of Wilfred Burchett*, Cambridge University Press, pp.17–30.

Carr, Bob 2022, "The Israeli lobby and Labor", *Pearls and Irritations*, 1 June. https://johnmenadue.com/the-lobby-and-labor/

Cohen, Mitchell 1992, *Zion and State: Nation, Class and the Shaping of Modern Israel*, Columbia University Press.

European Union 2024, "2023 Report on Israeli settlements in the occupied West Bank, including East Jerusalem Reporting period January–December 2023", 2 August. https://www.eeas.europa.eu/delegations/palestine-occupied-palestinian-territory-west-bank-and-gaza-strip/2023-report-israeli-settlements-occupied-west-bank-including-east-jerusalem-january-december-2023_en

Evatt, Herbert 1949, *The Task of Nations*, Greenwood Press.

Gibson, Ralph 1945, "Communists discuss problems of the Jewish People", *The Voice*, August.

Gibson, Ralph 1948, *War in Palestine*, International Bookshop for Victorian State Committee, Australian Communist Party. https://www.reasoninrevolt.net.au/objects/pdf/d0105.pdf

Glazer, SA 2007, "Language of Propaganda: The Histadrut, Hebrew labor, and the Palestinian worker", *Journal of Palestine Studies*, 36 (2), pp.25–38. https://www.proquest.com/scholarly-journals/language-propaganda-histadrut-hebrew-labor/docview/220627690/se-2

Gouttman, Rodney 1987, "First principles: HV Evatt and the Jewish homeland", in WD Rubenstein (ed.), *Jews in the Sixth Continent*, Allen and Unwin.

Harris, Marty 2012, "Australia and the Middle East conflict: a history of key Government statements (1947–2007)", 13 August. https://parlinfo.aph.gov.au/parlInfo/download/library/prspub/1845738/upload_binary/1845738.pdf

Hawke, Robert 1987a, "Transcript of Press Conference, King David Hotel, Jerusalem, 28 January 1987", *PM Transcripts*, Australian Government. https://pmtranscripts.pmc.gov.au/release/transcript-7089

Hawke, Robert 1987b, "Speech by the Prime Minister: anniversary of the Central Synagogue, Bondi Junction, 22 February 1987", *PM Transcripts*, Australian Government. https://pmtranscripts.pmc.gov.au/release/transcript-7126

Herzl, Theodor 1988 [1946], *The Jewish State*, Dover Publications, Inc. https://www.gutenberg.org/files/25282/25282-h/25282-h.htm#II_The_Jewish_Question

Karp, Paul 2024, "Pro-Palestine protests closing MPs' electorate offices 'have no place in a democracy', Albanese says", *The Guardian*, 4 June. https://www.theguardian.com/australia-news/article/2024/jun/04/pro-palestine-protests-targeting-mps-electorate-offices-have-no-place-in-a-democracy-albanese-says

Karpf, Anne 2002, "We've been here before", *The Guardian*, 8 June. https://www.theguardian.com/uk/2002/jun/08/immigration.immigrationandpublicservices

Knott, Matthew 2024, "Labor senators condemn 'river to the sea' chant in Fatima Payman rebuke", *The Guardian*, 16 May. https://www.smh.com.au/politics/federal/not-appropriate-albanese-criticises-labor-mp-over-israel-comments-20240516-p5je2s.html

Laing, Kate 2023, *Sisters in Peace: The Women's International League for Peace and Freedom in Australia, 1915–2015*, ANU Press. http://doi.org/10.22459/SP.2023

Lenin, Vladimir 1920, *Imperialism, the Highest Stage of Capitalism*, Preface to the French and German editions. https://www.marxists.org/archive/lenin/works/1916/imp-hsc/pref02.htm

Lockman, Zachary 1976, "The Left in Israel: Zionism vs. Socialism", *MERIP Reports*, 49, July, pp.3–19. https://doi.org/10.2307/3011124

Lockman, Zachary 1996, *Comrades and Enemies: Arab and Jewish Workers in Palestine, 1906–1948*, University of California Press.

Kramer, Martin 2017, "Who Saved Israel in 1947?", *Mosaic Magazine*, 6 November. https://scholar.harvard.edu/files/martinkramer/files/who_saved_israel_1947.pdf

Mendes, Philip 2009, "The Australian left's support for the creation of the state of Israel, 1947–48", *Labour History*, 97, pp.137–48.

Moor, Ahmed 2024, "Netanyahu's Theater of the Grotesque", *The Nation*, 25 July. https://www.thenation.com/article/world/netanyahus-theater-of-the-grotesque/

Peace Now 2023, "30 Years After Oslo – The data that shows how the settlements proliferated following the Oslo Accords", 11 September. https://peacenow.org.il/en/30-years-after-oslo-the-data-that-shows-how-the-settlements-proliferated-following-the-oslo-accords

Reich, Chanan 2002, *Australia and Israel*, Melbourne University Press.

Rothfield, Evelyn 1947, *Whither Palestine*, Dolphin Publications.

Rothfield, Evelyn 1948, *Israel Reborn*, Dolphin Publications.

Rubenstein, Colin and Tzvi Fleischer 2007, "A distant affinity: the history of Australian-Israeli relations", *Jewish Political Studies Review*, 19 (3–4), Fall. https://jcpa.org/article/a-distant-affinity-the-history-of-australian-israeli-relations-2/

Rubinstein, WD 1991, *The Jews in Australia: A Thematic History – Vol. 2, 1945 to the Present*, William Heinemann.

Rutland, Suzanne D 1990, "The Jewish Connection", in Heather Radi (ed.), *Jessie Street: Documents and Essays*, Women's Redress Press, pp.147–63.

Said, Edward 1993, "The Morning After", *London Review of Books*, 15 (20), 21 October. https://www.lrb.co.uk/the-paper/v15/n20/edward-said/the-morning-after

Segev, Tom 2019, *A state at any cost: the life of David Ben-Gurion*. Translated by Haim Watzman. Farrar, Straus and Giroux.

Slucki, David 2018, chapter 5, "New Frontiers", in *The International Jewish Labor Bund After 1945: Toward a Global History*, Rutgers University Press.

Sparrow, Jeff 2021, "Secret embassy cables cast the Bob Hawke legend in a different light", *The Guardian*, 3 July. https://www.theguardian.com/commentisfree/2021/jul/03/secret-embassy-cables-cast-the-bob-hawke-legend-in-a-different-light

Stalin, JV 1913, *Marxism and the National Question*. https://www.marxists.org/reference/archive/stalin/works/1913/03a.htm

Sternhell, Zeev 1998, *Founding Myths of Zionism*, Princeton University Press.

Thornton, Ernest 1945, "Palestine resolution and the World Trade Union Congress", *The Voice*, July, p.4.

Watts, Max 2004, "Fast memories [Howard Fast]", *Overland*, 175, June, pp.108–9. https://overland.org.au/wp-content/uploads/2023/06/175-2004.pdf

Weller, Patrick and Beverly Lloyd (eds) 1978, *Federal Executive Minutes 1915–1955: minutes of the meetings of the Federal Executive of the Australian Labor Party*, Melbourne University Press.

Whitlam, Gough 1985, *The Whitlam Government: 1972–1975*, Viking.

Wong, Penny 2023, "Remarks to the Australia-Israel Chamber of Commerce", 11 October 2023. https://www.foreignminister.gov.au/minister/penny-wong/speech/remarks-australia-israel-chamber-commerce

TOM BRAMBLE[1]

Empty promises: the ANC's failure to deliver freedom in South Africa

Tom Bramble has published widely on political economy and the labour movement and is a regular contributor to *Marxist Left Review*. His recent books include *Introducing Marxism: A Theory of Social Change* and *The Fight for Workers' Power: Revolution and Counter-Revolution in the 20th Century* (with Mick Armstrong).

SOUTH AFRICA'S SUBMISSION to the International Court of Justice accusing Israel of committing war crimes in Gaza in 2023 stirred an enormous wave of support within the international Palestine solidarity movement. That the US secretary of state denounced the case as "meritless" and "galling" only confirmed support for the country's African National Congress (ANC) government. The ANC's action seemed to confirm the special place South Africa has in the hearts of progressive people worldwide who recall its decades-long struggle to smash apartheid, the system of white supremacy that prevailed for most of the twentieth century founded on the form that capitalism took in this country. The government itself evoked this memory, with Minister of International Relations and Cooperation Naledi Pandor stating:

> South Africa has a moral responsibility to always stand with the oppressed because we come from a history of struggle, a history of striving for freedom, a history of believing that everybody deserves human dignity, justice and freedom; this is the only reason that we have taken this major step as South Africa.[2]

1. Thanks to Kate Alexander for helpful feedback on an earlier draft of this article.
2. Cited in McKinley 2024.

Fine words.

However, the notion that the ANC government represents a shining example of moral courage and support for the oppressed is belied by its actions at home. This was proven just a few months later when the ANC registered a dramatic loss in support at the May 2024 election, its vote tumbling from 57 percent in 2019 to just 40 percent. The ANC formed a coalition government with the Democratic Alliance (DA), Inkatha Freedom Party (IFP), Patriotic Alliance and the Freedom Front Plus, none of which could be labelled progressive.[3]

The 2024 election marks a further step in the erosion of the ANC's hegemony among those it once led in the struggle against apartheid and its aftermath. This is the result of its failure to confront the injustices of apartheid. While living standards for most of the oppressed black population rose in the first decade or two after the fall of apartheid, this process has since gone into reverse.

The failure of the ANC government to deliver for the mass of black people should not have been a surprise. Its rhetoric may have changed over the decades, but it has always been a party committed to capitalism. The transition to democracy in South Africa transformed the political shell, enshrined in what the ANC boasts as one of the most democratic constitutions in the world, but it left the basic economic structure intact, fixing grinding poverty and mass unemployment in place.

How apartheid in South Africa was smashed has lessons for freedom struggles today, not least for Palestine. The South African experience shows us that unless capitalism is overthrown, the outcome barely challenges the conditions of life for the working class and poor. The fight must be for socialism if justice is to prevail.

In the first half of this article, I will explain how the ANC steered the mass struggle of the 1980s into negotiations over constitutional reform that eliminated the apartheid superstructure but kept the fundamentals of South African capitalism intact. The second half will examine what this meant for the capitalists, middle class and working class since the advent of democracy.

---

3. Several micro parties also joined the government of national unity, but these were the ANC's main partners.

I The transition

The balance of forces in the mid-1980s[4]

During the 1980s, the working class in South Africa was on the march. New independent and non-racial unions were striking in massive numbers. The township youth were attacking the police and security forces, weakening the grip of the National Party (NP) government led by President PW Botha. The government faced a systemic crisis in the structures of apartheid, which meant that the apartheid regime could not continue to rule in the same old way. Nor was the working class willing to accept being ruled in that manner.

The apartheid government tried various methods to defeat the insurgency. It did its best to foster a network of collaborators among the non-white population. It also started modest reforms in the apartheid system of managing the working class, granting skilled black workers residency rights in the cities and making space for registered trade unions organised on a non-racial basis, hoping they might abandon demands for broader political transformation.

These manoeuvres failed. The black youth and workers rallied to the ANC and United Democratic Front (UDF) call to make the country ungovernable. The independent trade unions that registered with the government used the legal space opened to draw in still wider layers of the working class and organise them in militant strikes. The reforms failed because they attempted to make only minor adjustments to apartheid at a time when South Africa's economy increasingly relied on black labour, and black workers and students were becoming unwilling to accept their inferior position.

The regime struck back in 1986 after two years of mass strikes and township revolts. It declared two successive states of emergency, the second much more brutal than the first, resulting in an estimated 30,000 people being detained under emergency regulations. It also imposed numerous bans on oppositional groups, including the

---

4. The following analysis rests heavily on McKinley 1997 and Ceruti 2021.

ANC-led umbrella organisation, the UDF.[5] In response, the Congress of South African Trade Unions (Cosatu) mobilised two national stay-aways in 1988, each involving three million.[6] The government fought back, raiding Cosatu offices and imposing still wider bans, taking thousands more out of action. Legal repression was accompanied by vigilante attacks, break-ins, firebombing, assassinations and kidnapping in a trend that was only to accelerate in the following years. The government's repression was, for a time, successful. Democratic structures of resistance were destroyed in some areas and in others severely damaged. The result by early 1989 was "a mood of political quiescence", according to Eddie Webster and Maggie Friedman.[7] The regime had survived, but its reliance on states of emergency revealed its instability and the potential for fresh explosions of popular struggle. The status quo could not continue.

The other factor weighing on the apartheid regime in the mid-1980s was economic stagnation. The declining fortunes of the mining sector were key. For much of the twentieth century, government repression of black mineworkers, in particular gold miners whose labour underpinned the country's economy, kept wages low. The high profits extracted from mining drew in foreign investment and multimillion-dollar loans from the World Bank and Western banks, which were used to power the country's racially defined state capitalist development model, including infrastructure and manufacturing. In the late 1960s, the goldfields reached peak production, but in the following 15 years, the country experienced two sharp recessions triggered by falling gold prices. The economy pulled out of recession in 1983, but national output stagnated for the following decade, and the rand dropped from US$1.28 to 38 US cents between 1980 and 1990. The government responded with free-market reforms, eroding the old Afrikaner state capitalist edifice.

Here, the political and economic crises intertwined. Mass sackings

---

5. "Bans" could be imposed by the government without trial and declared the targeted organisation illegal or the individual ineligible to participate in political activity, often involving restrictions on their movement or right to associate with others.
6. A stay-away is a political general strike where activists close township entrances and set up pickets to enforce a boycott of work.
7. Cited in Ceruti 2021, p.97.

in the state-owned enterprises squeezed not just the white working and middle classes but also skilled black workers whose loyalty the regime had hoped to win. The project of creating an aspirational and loyal black working class was stillborn. Recognising that their investments were now at risk from the rebellious working class and growing economic difficulties, Western investors began to revisit their support for apartheid. Starting in 1983, when the IMF cut loans to South Africa, the big New York and London banks began to withdraw steadily, forcing the government to temporarily suspend debt repayments.

In September 1985, open divisions emerged within South Africa's ruling class when Gavin Relly, the chief executive of Anglo-American, the country's corporate behemoth, met with ANC leadership in Zambia, accompanied by other business leaders and newspaper editors. Relly was pleased with what he found, telling reporters that the ANC appeared "less militant than expected" and that there was a shared understanding of the need for a "cohesive and sensible" future for South Africa.[8]

Hoping to secure their interests regardless of whether apartheid continued or ended, South African capitalists began building relationships with the ANC. Their main goal was to persuade the ANC to drop its support for nationalisation and instead embrace a neoliberal approach. These overtures were reciprocated, resulting in the creation of the Consultative Business Movement to strengthen ties between business and the ANC.

While the business community supported the government's state of emergency, they sought political solutions that would eliminate the need for such crisis measures. Representative of the Federated Chamber of Industries, Bokkie Botha, told the *South African Labour Bulletin* in early 1988:

> There is no doubt from a businessman's point of view you cannot operate in an unrest situation. It's disruptive. So there is a belief that we need to contain unrest [but] at the same time you have to find a solution that allows people to talk... We are extremely

---

8. Cowell 1985.

concerned that the real voice of the people is being restricted, and the result is to develop a new underground.[9]

These were the circumstances driving the apartheid regime to consider more substantial reforms that ultimately led to its dissolution.

The National Party government flip-flopped between repression and reform in response to changing circumstances as debates raged between the "conservative" and "liberal" factions. Two things definitively tilted the balance towards reform. The first was a leadership change in January 1989 when Botha suffered a stroke, allowing FW De Klerk, regarded as a reformer within the NP, to take over as president. One of his first acts was to release five of those imprisoned alongside Nelson Mandela in 1962. This gave hope to the struggle organisations inside South Africa, which had been in such deep despondency only months earlier. Cosatu and the UDF organised open defiance of apartheid laws, including a three-million-strong stay-away against proposed elections for a fake tricameral parliament.

The second major event was the fall of the Berlin Wall in November 1989 and the disintegration of the Soviet bloc, which reshaped both local and global politics. For decades, the ruling classes in Britain and the US had seen South Africa as a reliable stronghold of Western imperialism in a region where Soviet- and Chinese-backed anti-colonial movements were making ground. However, with the collapse of the USSR, South Africa no longer served this geopolitical role, and the United States pushed the NP government to open negotiations with the ANC to try to stabilise the situation.

The ANC also faced an impasse. Its strategy of armed struggle had failed to undermine the apartheid state. It could not have been otherwise. South Africa was unlike Rhodesia (Zimbabwe) or Angola, where guerrilla forces could establish liberated areas and launch raids on rural centres. South Africa had a modern urban economy, and its military, the South African Defence Forces (SADF), was strong and united, relying on conscripted white servicemen. Even though white farmers were a minority, they controlled the rural black population and

---

9. Cited in Ceruti 2021, p.106.

acted as reservists for a vast military network. The ANC's military wing, uMkhonto we Sizwe (MK), could not set up guerrilla bases inside South Africa and could only carry out small-scale sabotage operations that netted few results.

Lacking internal bases, MK relied on neighbouring newly independent governments, but by the mid-1980s, the apartheid regime had struck deals with those states, most notably Mozambique, the only country from which MK had launched attacks on South Africa. These deals shut down MK bases and cut off their weapon supply. Meanwhile, Soviet President Mikhail Gorbachev reduced Russia's support for the ANC, including military aid, and encouraged the ANC to negotiate with the apartheid regime.

At home, the attempt to make South Africa ungovernable in the townships had been battered by savage states of emergency. The defeat of the 1987 National Union of Mineworkers (NUM) strike, the biggest strike to date, dampened militancy in the trade unions.

Before moving forward, it is important to understand that while the ANC publicly emphasised armed struggle as a key part of its fight against apartheid – attracting some of the most determined young fighters – none of its leaders believed that armed struggle could overthrow the regime. The guerrilla campaign was merely a tactic to pressure the government into negotiating. This became clear in 1988–89 when the ANC released the Constitutional Guidelines and the Harare Declaration. These outlined the ANC's commitment to a negotiated transition to democracy that would preserve the dominance of big business. The fall of the Berlin Wall gave leaders of the South African Communist Party (SACP) the political cover they needed to abandon the goal of socialism in South Africa, even as a distant possibility.

Nature of the ANC – historic overview

The fact that the ANC and its alliance partner, the SACP, were not interested in socialism in South Africa might challenge the assumptions of some readers. Many ANC leaders were SACP members and occasionally declared their support for socialism, especially when speaking to working-class audiences. The apartheid regime and its international supporters had always described the ANC as a communist threat.

However, the ANC was never interested in socialist transformation in South Africa. It had always been a pro-capitalist organisation. The early ANC leaders were very moderate in their approach. Influenced by their Christian education, they aimed to convince the British that property-owning and educated Africans should be included in South African society. They aimed to widen the limited voting rights available to property-owning black Africans in the Cape. They sent delegations to London to urge the British government to repeal the Natives Land Act, which allocated the black population just 13 percent of the land. The British were unmoved. As a result, the ANC leaders became disheartened, and the organisation began to fall apart in the 1920s. In the 1930s, ANC leaders ignored the growing unrest among the black working class, whose demands conflicted with their desire for modest changes to civil rights. During World War II, the ANC backed the British government and the Smuts coalition government in Pretoria which mobilised more than 300,000 South Africans for the war effort, including more than 100,000 black people, Coloureds and Indians.[10]

The Communist Party of South Africa (CPSA), as it was then known, was in thrall to Moscow in the 1930s. It propounded a Stalinist popular front strategy in which all social classes, except the most reactionary, could unite to fight for national liberation, the first stage of what was deemed a two-stage revolution, with the latter stage the eventual triumph of socialism. The corollary was that working-class interests were set aside in favour of those amenable to the party's putative allies, including "progressive" white labour, "liberal" British and international capital and African nationalists.

The CPSA followed every twist and turn coming out of Moscow. On the outbreak of World War II, the CPSA opposed it and attacked the Smuts government for its support for Britain, which was in line with Stalin's 1939 pact with Hitler. Only following the Nazi invasion of Russia in 1941 did the party switch to supporting the British war effort,

---

10. No study of South African history can avoid using the racial categories entrenched by the apartheid regime. The term "Coloured" was used to refer to "mixed race" South Africans. Despite its objectionable history, the term was adopted widely by Coloured people and is used today without pejorative intent. The first letter of the racial descriptor "black" is commonly written in lowercase, not capitalised as it is in the United States.

arguing that it was now a war for democracy against fascism. The party now did its best, not always successfully, to rein in strikes.

Black workers continued to fight, however, even during wartime. After the war ended, 70,000 gold mine workers on the Witwatersrand struck. The Smuts government violently crushed the strike, killing 13 workers, injuring 1,250 and arresting over 1,000. The strike brought home to the South African ruling class, both English-speaking and Afrikaners, the need to suppress black labour. They embraced even harsher measures to control the movement of black labour and limit the development of a settled black urban working class, which would have posed a major threat. In the 1948 election, the pro-apartheid National Party and its allies, benefiting from a highly gerrymandered whites-only election, defeated the Smuts coalition government, mobilising its support base among white farmers.

The defeat of the miners' strike was a decisive setback that weakened the whole labour movement – white and black – and severely limited the mass resistance to the imposition of formal apartheid after 1948.

With the confidence of the black working class hit hard, African nationalism received a boost. This was the program of black professionals and small capitalists frustrated by their political and economic marginalisation by the apartheid regime and who were prepared to support more confrontational tactics than the ANC had pursued hitherto. This was the context in which the ANC Youth League, led by Mandela, Anton Lembede, Robert Sobukwe, Walter Sisulu and Oliver Tambo, won control of the ANC in 1949, forcing out the old guard. In place of polite petitioning, they argued for direct action and mass mobilisation, including active boycotts, stay-aways, civil disobedience and non-cooperation. These tactics enthused many black people threatened by the NP government's increasingly draconian restrictions.

African nationalism served a useful purpose for the ANC since it could inspire the majority of poor and oppressed black South Africans to join the fight against apartheid while limiting their demands for full social, economic, and political freedom that could have undermined the ANC's efforts to secure power for themselves, and the layer of middle-class black professionals and black capitalists they represented.

This dual orientation overlapped with that of the predominantly white Communist Party. The party had been banned by the National Party government in 1950 and voted to dissolve but then reformed as an underground organisation, the SACP, in 1953. Black Communists had been active in the ANC since the 1930s, but the SACP now threw itself more deeply behind the ANC, which it determined to be the leading force of the national democratic revolution.[11] The SACP brought with it not just a Stalinist theoretical apparatus to justify class collaboration but also Stalinist organisational methods to what had been rather ramshackle ANC structures. In 1955, the party recruited Sisulu, and in 1960, Mandela. Soon after joining, both were elected or drafted onto the SACP central committee.

The 1955 Freedom Charter, largely written by the SACP's Rusty Bernstein, embodied the delicate balancing act attempted by the ANC and its Communist supporters. The Charter was the work of the newly formed Congress Alliance, comprising the ANC and the heavily Communist-influenced white Congress of Democrats, the South African Coloured Organisation, the South African Indian Congress, the South African Council of Trade Unions (SACTU) and the predominantly white Federation of South African Women.

Stating that South Africa belongs to "all who live in it" and calling for "a democratic state, based on the will of the people", the Charter set out a list of demands:

- the people shall govern
- all national groups shall have equal rights
- the people shall share in the country's wealth
- the land shall be shared among those who work it
- all shall be equal before the law
- all shall enjoy equal human rights
- there shall be work and security
- the doors of learning and culture shall be opened
- there shall be houses, security and comfort
- there shall be peace and friendship.

11. The ANC opened membership to all races in 1985, before which time its membership was exclusively black.

There was enough in the Charter to appeal to the black working class and poor farmers. But it was also helpfully ambiguous. The demand that "the people shall share in the country's wealth" could be understood by the ANC's working-class supporters and capitalist opponents as tantamount to wholesale nationalisation. At the same time, for African nationalists, it could mean a post-apartheid state overseeing a mixed economy in which both state and private capital played a role.[12] But the ANC leadership was never in doubt about its real purpose. Mandela explained in 1956 that the ANC's goal was to empower a new black bourgeoisie that would prosper once the white capitalists were expropriated:

> The breaking up and democratisation of these [bank, mining and land] monopolies will open up fresh fields for the development of a prosperous non-European bourgeois class. For the first time in the history of this country the non-European bourgeoisie will have the opportunity to own, in their own name and right, mines and factories, and trade and private enterprise will boom and flourish as never before.[13]

Workers' power was not on the agenda, Mandela made clear:

> The Charter does not contemplate such profound [socialist] economic and political challenges. Its declaration "The People Shall Govern" visualises the transfer of power not to any single social class but to all the people of the country, be they workers, peasants, professional men or petty-bourgeoisie.[14]

During the 1950s, the ANC leadership embarked on tightly controlled demonstrations, passive resistance, stay-aways, and strikes to force the National Party government to open talks. The government flatly

---

12. McKinley 1997, p.21.
13. Significantly, the SACP's Ruth First deleted this paragraph from Mandela's article when the party subsequently republished it in the 1960s as it made the ANC's project rather too plain.
14. Mandela 1956.

rebuffed them and, in 1956, charged 156 Congress Alliance leaders and activists with treason, tying them up in court cases for years before they were finally acquitted in 1961.

The ANC also faced pressure on another flank from the newly formed Pan-Africanist Congress (PAC). Robert Sobukwe, one of the country's best-known black leaders, split from the ANC in 1959 and took many of the ANC's leading cadres to form the PAC. The new organisation argued for a more thoroughgoing African nationalist program, an end to working with communists from white, Indian and Coloured backgrounds and a more confrontational approach to the authorities. Following the Sharpeville massacre in March 1960, in which the security forces killed 69 protesters demanding an end to the pass laws that prevented free movement of black people, the PAC started to prepare for armed struggle and drew young militants to its ranks attracted by its radical rhetoric.

In December 1960, a meeting of SACP leaders, including Mandela, having assured itself of Soviet and Chinese support in the form of weapons and training, adopted the armed struggle tactic and instructed the central committee to prepare for the use of force. The first communist sabotage unit was formed in the first half of 1961, and in December 1961 the organisation, now named MK, launched sabotage actions in Johannesburg, Cape Town and Durban. Initially refusing to endorse the SACP initiative, the ANC officially recognised MK as its armed wing in 1962.

The sabotage campaign represented a sharp turn by the SACP and ANC, but it amounted to little more than pinpricks in the machinery of apartheid. It gave the regime an excuse to clamp down harder on internal dissent. MK had hardly been established when, in July 1963, almost the entire leadership of the ANC and MK were arrested at MK headquarters in Rivonia, with most sentenced to life imprisonment.

The shift to armed struggle and the violent repression by the apartheid regime had several long-lasting effects on the ANC's actions in the following decades. First, it forced the ANC to move its operations outside South Africa, with Oliver Tambo establishing a headquarters in Dar es Salaam, Tanzania. Second, by strengthening the ANC's ties to the Soviet Union and other Eastern Bloc countries, it raised the SACP's profile.

The SACP 1962 document, "The Road to South African Freedom", set out the party's pseudo-socialist theoretical underpinning. The party characterised apartheid as "colonialism of a special type" (CST). This theory claimed that two separate modes of production existed side by side in South Africa: a modern capitalist white economy and a semi-feudal black economy. According to this view, black South Africa was a colony of its white oppressors. Colonial oppression, not capitalism, was the enemy and must be overthrown through a national democratic revolution led by the multi-class liberation movement. The working class, the SACP to the fore, was held up as the critical revolutionary force pushing national liberation and eventually leading the fight for socialism, but workers must understand that this latter stage would come many years after the former.

CST was bunkum, no more than a smokescreen for the SACP's counter-revolutionary project. South Africa was an integrated capitalist economy, and black labour was fundamental to its operation. There was no reason for any uprising by black workers to halt once having smashed the legal structures of apartheid; the fight against racial oppression and the struggle for working-class emancipation could, under the right leadership, be one and the same.

The SACP's counter-revolutionary character explains why it talked a great deal about the working class in the 1960s and 1970s but did little to organise working-class struggle. Instead, it gave left-wing cover to the ANC that primarily represented the interests of the black bourgeoisie and petty bourgeoisie. In 1969, the ideological continuity between the two organisations was confirmed when the ANC adopted much of the SACP's "The Road to South African Freedom", including CST, in its platform.

As the ANC's operations shifted beyond South Africa's borders and its ties to the Soviet Bloc deepened, its leaders increasingly relied on international diplomacy to pressure the apartheid regime. In 1961–62, Mandela and fellow MK leader Joe Slovo visited East Germany, Algeria, Ghana, Tanzania and Zambia to seek support for their cause.

Secretly hatched military operations involving small numbers of fighters sidelined mass action. SACP member and MK leader Ben Turok later noted of the turn to armed struggle:

> Sabotage had the effect of isolating the organised movement from the mass who felt unable to join in this new phase or even to defend the actionists when they were seized... The sabotage campaign failed on the main count – it did not raise the level of action of the masses themselves... they were left on the threshold, frustrated bystanders of a battle being waged on their behalf.[15]

The ANC's turn to armed struggle, combined with the growing influence of Stalinism, reinforced an authoritarian culture within the organisation, where internal disagreements were often resolved through imprisoning opponents in harsh camp prisons or even executing them.

The ANC's external orientation explains why the ANC had little political impact inside South Africa during the 1960s, even as the apartheid regime forcibly drove millions of black residents from the cities and arrested those who resisted. So it was that when internal struggles resurfaced after a decade of inactivity, the ANC was caught unprepared. The first breakthrough came with the 1973 Durban strikes and the rise of independent trade unions, which formed the Federation of South African Trade Unions (Fosatu) in 1979. Fosatu brought together a new working-class vanguard of workers in metal and engineering, automotive, paper and wood, rubber, chemicals, glass, food, transport, stevedoring, and textiles and clothing. The leaders, veteran unionists, younger workers and student activists were radical syndicalists. Having witnessed the subordination of trade unions by other bourgeois and petty bourgeois African liberation movements, Fosatu's leaders understood the importance of maintaining political independence from the ANC.

The ANC and SACP greeted the new unions with hostility. They accused them of collaborating with apartheid because they used the regime's legal mechanisms for collective bargaining to organise strikes and secure higher wages and better conditions for workers. Their main

---

15. Cited in McKinley 1997, p.32.

objection was that the new unions represented a challenge to the ANC's authority over the black working class.

The ANC was also caught off guard by the rising militancy among black students and intellectuals in the 1970s, reflected in the growing popularity of the Black Consciousness movement. The ANC was initially absent from the 1976 Soweto uprising when the township's school students protested being compelled to learn in Afrikaans and were met with brutal repression by the security forces, Inkatha thugs and black vigilante groups sponsored by the authorities. Hundreds were killed over the following 12 months. Although Black Consciousness did not form a stable political organisation, its central slogan, "Black man, you are on your own!" resonated deeply with the students in Soweto, who felt that no one would save them but themselves.

While the ANC could not initially respond positively to these developments, the party eventually caught up. Without any opposition from an organised revolutionary party, the ANC eventually regained the influence it had lost in the 1960s. After the township revolts in Soweto and the Cape Flats were brutally suppressed, thousands of radicalised school students fled the country to join MK camps in Zambia. With "Marxism" linked to the Stalinist politics of the SACP, the chance to bring Black Consciousness supporters into genuine revolutionary politics was missed.

The next generation of township students was energised by the UDF's 1984 call to make South Africa ungovernable. They took to the streets, targeting security forces and township councillors seen as puppets and informers. However, these, too, lacked any political leadership independent of the ANC. Within a few years, the UDF came under the ANC's control and was dissolved in 1991 after a period of inactivity, marking the ANC's decision to prioritise negotiations over mass struggle.

The same process of absorption took place with the independent unions. The syndicalist union leaders rejected forming a radical working-class political party to challenge the Congress Alliance. This, however, only allowed the latter to impose its political project on them. This became clear with the township stay-aways in the 1980s organised under the auspices of the United Democratic Front. The Fosatu unions alternated between abstaining from the stay-aways because they did not involve on-the-job struggles and simply tailing the ANC. The relationship between the independent unions and the ANC was still unresolved in 1985 when Fosatu unions dissolved the federation to become founding members of Cosatu. Within two years, however, the Cosatu leaders joined the Congress Alliance, acknowledging the leading role of the ANC in the name of the national democratic revolution.

By the late 1980s, the ANC had firmly established itself as the uncontested leader of the anti-apartheid movement. For those disappointed with the ANC's limited goals, the SACP offered a left-sounding rationale. Many believed the SACP might push for socialism and joined the party on that basis, but that was never its plan.

Contested transition

The period between Mandela's release from jail and the ANC's election victory is sometimes described as a "managed transition", when the National Party and ANC smoothly transitioned South Africa from apartheid to democracy. However, this oversimplifies the reality. The transition was far from smooth, and the outcome was uncertain. Neither the National Party nor the ANC initially expected the process to result in a full parliamentary democracy, a relatively liberal constitution, or the eventual dissolution of the National Party.[16]

The transition to democracy went further than either party anticipated, mainly due to pressure from below. The 1986 State of Emergency demonstrated that the internal security apparatus remained intact and could still strike hard against the movement. The working class lacked revolutionary leadership and did not establish any organs of workers' power. However, if the working class could not seize power, it played an important role at critical moments, pushing the transition forward, strengthening the ANC's negotiating position and forcing the National Party to make more concessions.

In February 1990, President De Klerk announced the unbanning of the ANC and other illegal political organisations, and Mandela was released from prison. In May, a four-year process of discussions began

---

16. The material that follows rests heavily on Ceruti 2021.

between the two adversaries, a precondition of which was the ANC's acceptance of a negotiated settlement. In August, the ANC unilaterally suspended armed struggle without receiving any concessions, to the dismay of Cosatu and the SACP, partners in what was now dubbed the Tripartite Alliance.

At the same time, the government increased its support for the right-wing Zulu nationalist Inkatha led by KwaZulu Bantustan chief executive Mangosuthu Buthelezi as part of its strategy to weaken the ANC.[17] Inkatha launched violent attacks on ANC strongholds in Johannesburg's townships and hostels, trying to extend its influence into the Transvaal. While the ANC verbally supported communities defending themselves against Inkatha, it did not organise self-defence efforts. Only Cosatu took action, mobilising three million people for a stay-away protest against the violence in July 1990.

In February 1991, after declaring it "the year of mass action for people's power", the ANC organised large marches in Cape Town and Pretoria during the opening of the white Parliament. However, these actions were mainly used to strengthen the ANC's negotiating position. The National Party, committed to retaining as much as possible of apartheid structures and fearing loss of support to white parties further to its right, was slow to make concessions. Meanwhile, Inkatha's attacks grew more intense. Only the revelation that the government had been funding Inkatha, enabling it to carry out murderous attacks on ANC supporters, pushed the government back in the face of public outrage at its duplicity. This led to a peace accord meant to disarm Inkatha, but the group ignored the agreement, and the violence continued.

It was not until November 1991 that the violence eased temporarily, when Cosatu organised a two-day stay-away involving three million people to protest the introduction of a Value Added Tax (VAT). Although the stay-away momentarily halted the violence, it did not

---

17. Bantustans were impoverished and ethnically defined "homelands" for millions of displaced black people forcibly removed from cities or fertile rural areas by the apartheid regime to enforce the migrant labour system and deny black people South African citizenship and political rights. They were ruled by local chiefs who were mostly clients of the Pretoria regime, although some, such as Buthelezi, vacillated between support and opposition depending on whichever offered advantages at the time.

signal an alternative to the ongoing negotiations. It served more to show the government that it could not unilaterally impose significant economic changes without facing resistance.

Negotiations started in December 1991 with the first Conference for a Democratic South Africa (CODESA), a process heavily stacked against the anti-apartheid movement with just three delegations out of 19. In August 1992, Cosatu called a nationwide stay-away. This was a tremendous success, with four million staying away from work and school. This forced the NP to back down on its initial resistance. It conceded a sovereign constituent assembly and elections by the end of 1993 and an interim government to oversee them, even if, in the following months, it did its best to limit these concessions as much as it could.

The ANC negotiators needed episodes of mass action to break NP foot-dragging, but they were also acutely aware that as a government-in-waiting, they were to inherit a South Africa where none of the vast inequalities and oppressions had been resolved and where workers had shown they were prepared to fight for their rights. Mass action could be turned on, but for their futures, it must also be turned off when necessary. Thus, the ANC argued that rolling mass action was

> not a programme for insurrection. ... There is a growing realisation that this task [of reconstruction] belongs to all South Africans. After all, a climate of fear, uncertainty and a lack of investor confidence affects ordinary people's lives as much as it undermines productivity and disrupts the whole economy.[18]

The SACP agreed. The priority was to win control of the state as a platform to fight for further gradual advances, aka the national democratic revolution, even if that meant power-sharing. Not everyone in the Tripartite Alliance was convinced. The ANC Youth League argued:

> A study of the short record of negotiations does not give evidence that we have made any gains by making compromises... There is

---

18. Cited in Ceruti 2021, p.116.

more evidence that the breakthroughs we have made so far have been the result of unrelenting struggles.[19]

The importance of mass struggle was reinforced following the assassination of popular SACP and MK leader Chris Hani in April 1993. In the months leading up to the murder, negotiations between the ANC and NP government had stalled, with no concrete steps to prepare for democratic elections. Impatience with the negotiations within the ANC's constituency was building. Hani's murder by a far-right assassin, provided with a gun by a Conservative Party MP, blew the lid off the pressure cooker. Big protests erupted in townships and urban centres across the country. Thousands took to the streets, with many demonstrations turning violent as frustrations boiled over. Black youths blamed their leaders for allowing them to be led like lambs to the slaughter; "Give us guns", they cried. Fearing that the explosion of anger might derail negotiations, Mandela stepped in, using his immense authority to appeal for "unity" and patience. To get to the head of the movement, the ANC called two stay-aways that were overwhelmingly observed in all the big cities, each accompanied by giant marches. On the day of Hani's funeral, tens of thousands of mourners attended, along with similar numbers elsewhere attending local events around the country. The ANC managed to steer its supporters off the streets and, in doing so, saved the negotiations. In return, the government was forced to set a date for the election one year hence.

As the April 1994 election approached, a new wave of mass struggle erupted. Right-wing Bantustan leaders, whom the apartheid regime had supported for decades, resisted the integration of their territories into a united, democratic South Africa. In Bophuthatswana, a mass uprising put an end to one such holdout. When leader Lucas Mangope refused to give up power, thousands of civilians flooded the streets of Mafikeng, destroying symbols of Bantustan authority. Even the police mutinied and joined the protests. Mangope called on white far-right militias for help. The militias rushed in, shooting protesters and bystanders. But the crowds, along with the rebellious police, fought

---

19. Cited in Ceruti 2021, p.117.

back, eventually driving the militias out, wounding and killing many of them. Mangope was forced to flee the capital.

When people in other Bantustans saw what happened in Bophuthatswana, they launched similar protests, and their leaders quickly gave up resisting reintegration. Although ANC activists were involved in these protests, the ANC leadership, worried about reviving the rebellious spirit of 1984, worked to calm things down. The ANC made a deal in KwaZulu, where Buthelezi threatened to boycott the election. They agreed to leave the Bantustan state and police force untouched – despite Buthelezi using them to attack ANC supporters in Natal and Transvaal – as the price for his cooperation in the new political order.

Finally, the dawn of a new age arrived when, after decades of struggle, the ANC won the May 1994 election, only narrowly missing a two-thirds majority that would have allowed it to change the interim constitution. It also won control of seven of the nine provinces. As part of the transition agreed by the ANC, the National Party and IFP joined it in a government of national unity, with De Klerk serving as vice president and Buthelezi as Home Affairs minister until 1996, when a new constitution was adopted.[20] The central state and regional governments reflected the apartheid legacy – managers and professionals running the public service were predominantly white. Likewise the SADF and state security forces, while MK veterans were, for the most part, simply abandoned.

If the ANC agreed to a string of political concessions that propped up the NP and IFP and afforded them a role far beyond their popular support, it also showed its willingness to placate local and international capitalists in the transition years. The Freedom Charter affirmed that "the people shall share in the country's wealth", and the ANC occasionally spoke about nationalising the big industries. But, starting in the late 1980s, as the prospect of a negotiated transition became reality, the ANC quickly confirmed its loyalty to the basic principles of capitalism.

Throughout the long years of struggle, the ANC never developed a clear economic plan, and neither did its allies, the SACP and Cosatu.

---

20. "Inkatha" was renamed the Inkatha Freedom Party (IFP) at the time of the 1994 election.

This created a gap that others moved to fill. Groups like Cosatu-linked Economic Trends and Industrial Strategy research teams, the Macroeconomic Research Group (MERG), and international bodies such as the London-based Economic Research on South Africa and the Centre for Research into Economics and Finance in Southern Africa stepped in. These groups explored different models, looking to Japan and South Korea for industrial and trade policies and Scandinavia for Keynesian welfare policies. Meanwhile, business aggressively lobbied the ANC to adopt their preferred policies.

These discussions led to the creation of the Transitional Executive Council, which included the government and the ANC, and the National Economic Forum, involving government, business, and labour. As the ANC moved closer to taking office and thus responsibility for managing South African capitalism, its economic policy drifted steadily to the right. It agreed to honour the country's $25 billion foreign debt and maintain the central bank's independence. In December 1993, it endorsed the NP government's decision to take out a $850m loan from the IMF with harsh conditions. It foreswore serious land reform. It enshrined property rights into the constitution and assured the capitalists that nationalisation was not part of its agenda. It also approved swingeing GATT tariff cuts that were to gut the manufacturing industry.

In 1992, with the country suffering a grinding recession, the ANC released its "Ready to Govern" document, which became the foundation for its 1994 election manifesto, the Reconstruction and Development Programme (RDP). There was nothing socialist about the RDP; it was designed to manage South Africa's capitalist system. Economic growth was expected to result from redistribution, creating a more stable domestic consumer base and making the economy less reliant on gold. The RDP did not aim to shift the balance of power between the working class and the capitalist class – capitalism was accepted as the default system. The RDP aimed to strengthen South Africa's position in that system.

The ANC's role became one of facilitating the changes that South African and international capitalists wanted but that the discredited National Party could not deliver. The SACP reassured those seeking deeper change by promising that the ANC in power would serve as a stepping stone for a more radical transformation. However, as events unfolded, it became clear that the ANC's victory was not the beginning of a move away from capitalism but rather its guarantor.

II The ANC record in office

Capitalists and middle class: change and continuity

Apartheid bequeathed South Africa appalling inequality. Racial disparities were enormous. Whites' average per capita income was double that of Indians, five times that of Coloureds and 7.5 times that of black people. While 62 percent of black people fell below a poverty line set at R250 pcm (in 1996 rands), only 3 percent of whites did.[21] The vast majority of black people were working class or rural poor. The black middle class, comprising teachers, nurses, priests, police, shopkeepers, taxi owners and a few professionals, constituted just 3 percent of the black population.[22] Black people were almost absent in government or public sector roles of any significance (outside the Bantustans), and few black people were company directors. Expectations were high among the millions who voted for the ANC in 1994 that democracy would lift the people out of poverty. This section will outline the main outcomes of three decades of ANC rule.

The most striking development of post-apartheid South Africa is that the upper reaches of the state apparatus have been transformed. The five presidents since 1994 have all been black.[23] Of the 34 ministers in the current government of national unity, all but six are black, and of the directors-general, all but one. All but one provincial premier is black, and black politicians now dominate legislatures in every province except the Western Cape. The upper ranks of the judicial system, including the chief justice, are black. The national police commissioner and all provincial police commissioners are black. Every one of the chiefs of the defence forces is black. Black vice chancellors

---

21. Hirsch et al 2022, p.69.
22. In South African parlance, "taxi" usually refers to minibuses, tens of thousands owned by companies competing, sometimes violently, for custom on set routes.
23. For the sake of simplicity in this paragraph, "black" here refers to black Africans, Coloureds and Indians, all three of whom were racially oppressed under apartheid.

lead the country's top universities. The head of the state broadcasting corporation is black, as is every member of the SABC board. The ANC's historic mission to raise black South Africans to leadership roles in the state apparatus has been fulfilled.

The ANC has tried to use state power to create a black capitalist class. As the National Party did with Afrikaners in earlier decades, the ANC has appointed loyalists to lead state-owned enterprises (SOEs) and parastatals. Keeping most parastatals in government hands has allowed the ANC to allocate jobs, management positions, investment and procurement opportunities to favoured insiders, which Roger Southall calls a "party-state bourgeoisie".[24] Corruption, particularly in government outsourcing and procurement, is endemic and referred to as "tenderpreneurship" providing ample opportunity for organised crime to leech off the public purse.

Progress in building a black capitalist class in the private sector has been slower. Through black economic empowerment (BEE), the ANC has pushed white-run corporations, especially large mining companies, to appoint black board members, lend money to black businesspeople to buy shares, and give contracts to black-owned companies.[25] Phumzile Mlambo-Ngcuka, Mandela's deputy minister for trade and industry, set the tone early on by saying that "Blacks should not be ashamed to be 'filthy rich'".

BEE gained momentum under President Thabo Mbeki. In 1998, the new president created the BEE Commission, chaired by Cyril Ramaphosa, the former NUM leader and ANC secretary-general turned businessman. Its task was, as Mbeki put it, "promoting the formation of a Black Bourgeoisie which will itself be committed and contribute to BEE".[26] Corporations were eager to comply, seeing BEE as a way to gain favour with the government and influence policy. Key beneficiaries included Saki Macozoma, Patrice Motsepe, Cyril Ramaphosa and Tokyo Sexwale, three of whom were on the ANC national executive. These new black capitalists acquired equity stakes worth billions of

---

24. Southall 2014, p.655; Tangri and Southall 2008.
25. The account that follows is based on Vilakazi 2022.
26. Cited in Hirsch et al 2022, p.79.

rands in South Africa's top communications, banking, industrial and natural resources companies.

For those in the ANC's inner circle, BEE was a win-win. A small layer of black businesspeople became extremely wealthy, corporations secured favourable government contracts, and the ANC used BEE to raise funds for the party. There was an obvious tension, however. The big capitalists may have welcomed a few appointments to company boards and an offloading of what were often marginal parts of their businesses to black businesspeople. However, they strongly opposed a wholesale transfer of ownership of the type occurring in neighbouring Zimbabwe. And so, in 2002, when Mlambo-Ngcuka, now mines and energy minister, proposed black ownership of mining companies be lifted to 51 percent within ten years, the capitalists reacted, wiping billions of rands off the value of South Africa's mining stocks. The minister capitulated, halving the target and giving the mining companies veto powers over implementation.

The failure of BEE to spread money beyond a well-connected few sparked the most serious faction fight in the ANC's history, as Jacob Zuma rallied those in the party cadres demanding their share of the loot against Mbeki, whom they denounced as a slave to neoliberalism and "white monopoly capital". If the private sector would not deal them in, the SOEs must. Cynically holding the banner of "radical economic transformation" (RET) aloft, Zuma defeated Mbeki in the contest for ANC president at the party's 2007 conference and assumed the national presidency in 2009. Once president, Zuma set in train a wholesale transfer of national wealth to his supporters. SOE managers bent procurement rules to favour the well-connected. Zuma's relations with the wealthy Gupta family were only the most high-profile case. With the economy stagnating after 2014, open looting of public enterprises and kickbacks from private capitalists became the surest route to large fortunes. Scandal after scandal followed, involving thousands of ANC insiders and multinational business consultancies. The Gupta empire finally blew up when tens of thousands of private emails were leaked to investigative journalists. The Guptas fled to Dubai, and in 2018 Zuma was ousted as president by his long-serving deputy, Ramaphosa.

Ramaphosa promised a break from the corruption that marked

his predecessor's reign. But he did not have clean hands himself. He had amassed an enormous fortune as a politically connected business executive whose businesses were revealed as illicitly removing funds from the country. In 2012, as a director and significant shareholder of mining giant Lonmin, Ramaphosa pressured the police to take action that led to the murder of 34 striking mineworkers at the Marikana platinum mine in North West Province.

Ramaphosa's actions at Marikana confirm that black capitalists treat their workforces no better than their white predecessors. They have adopted the same methods to extract more value from their workers, using labour brokers to outsource employment and squeeze wages and conditions. One recent review concludes: "In practice, the main benefits of BEE programs in the mining industry went to a relatively small group of private black investors rather than communities, workers, or emerging new businesses".[27]

Further down the class hierarchy, the ANC has also used state power to promote a black middle class. The apartheid regime started this process hoping to divide the freedom fight but had little success outside the Bantustans. It is only since the fall of apartheid that a substantial black middle class has emerged, with Southall arguing that: "the party-state has become a – if not the – fulcrum around which upward social mobility and chances for 'private accumulation' revolve for historically disadvantaged segments of the population".[28]

Affirmative action programs have significantly increased educational opportunities in state secondary schools and higher education, particularly the well-resourced historically white institutions. In addition, equity employment programs in government, the professions, big corporations and the media have resulted in a degree of deracialisation in workplaces. Black people now constitute a much bigger share of the middle class. In 2016, 59 percent of the top income quintile were black, up from 34 percent in 2001, and the figure is likely higher today.[29] Many university-educated black professionals have moved into

---

27. Makgetla 2022, p.277.
28. Southall 2014, p.652.
29. Bredenkamp et al 2021.

previously all-white suburbs in the big cities.[30] The growing prosperity of the black middle class helps explain the marked growth of wage inequality *within* the black population since 1994.

Then there are the black business and trading bourgeoisie in medium and small companies, sometimes merging with the lumpenproletariat and organised crime sector, as is evident in the taxi and construction sectors, traditional strongholds of the black petty bourgeoisie.

The ANC has sought to use the growing black middle class as a buffer to protect it from the working class. For many years, the middle class complied. From 1994 to 2009, support for the ANC increased among black business owners and professionals.[31] In more recent elections, however, black middle-class support for the ANC has declined, but no other party has been able to capitalise on this. The Democratic Alliance (DA) has tried to attract this group, hoping that their rising affluence would shift their political loyalties. However, the DA's mostly white, conservative support base has discouraged many black middle-class voters from jumping ship to join the DA. The Economic Freedom Fighters (EFF), with its focus on the black poor, has not appealed to this group either. Other smaller parties have tried and scored derisory votes or failed to repeat initial success in subsequent elections, quickly fading to nothing. Those dissatisfied with the ANC have tended simply not to vote rather than rally behind a rival party.[32]

While the racial makeup of the political leadership and many professions has changed significantly since 1994, wealth and capital remain concentrated among a small number of white-owned conglomerates and family businesses.[33] By 2020, no black-owned companies were among the top firms listed on the Johannesburg Stock Exchange (JSE), and very few black-owned businesses had grown significantly. BEE has mostly not been an entry point for a black bourgeoise to start the process of capital accumulation but is mainly about sharing rents, along with targets in skills development, management and

---

30. Southall 2023.
31. Southall 2014, p.657.
32. Ndletyana 2024.
33. Vilakazi 2022, p.603.

procurement among the politically connected. This has reinforced the existing economic structure rather than changed it.

That so much of the country's economic base remains in the same hands as in the days of apartheid is the product of the ANC's commitment to capitalism. While it uses patronage to build a layer of loyalists and uses these connections to loot the SOEs for its purposes, the ANC also seeks the support of local and international big business. Investment in the productive sector is already very low, and the ANC fears that any more substantial redistribution will lead to massive capital flight.

The ANC's support for big business was apparent in 1996 when it abandoned the RDP and introduced a new plan, the Growth, Employment and Redistribution Program (GEAR). This promised cuts to the budget deficit, lower tariffs and corporate taxes, privatisation, further loosening foreign exchange controls, lower public sector wages and reduced inflation. GEAR signalled to financial markets and the ANC base that the government would not pursue progressive reforms.

A critical decision in 1999 allowed major companies to move their financial headquarters overseas. Anglo-American, De Beers and Gencor (a predecessor of BHP Billiton) shifted listings to London and Melbourne, becoming global players while shedding local operations and causing significant job losses. Other capitalists followed suit, acquiring properties abroad and merging with global giants. While shareholders benefited, the South African Treasury suffered as these firms minimised tax liabilities and paid foreign shareholders in hard currency, worsening the current account deficit.

The South African economy grew fairly steadily from 1994 until 2008 when it slumped dramatically during the global financial crisis. Economic growth has been feeble in the 15 years since, and per capita GDP is now lower than in 2012. Private investment has dwindled and state-owned enterprises have accrued substantial debts. Lack of basic infrastructure maintenance is causing recurrent power outages, water shortages and service disruptions. Mafia-like groups demanding "protection" money and waging violent turf wars are widespread in mining, construction and the taxi industry. Productivity is flat. Government debt has risen to 72 percent of GDP from 28 percent in

2008, and the rand has dropped from 28 US cents in 1994 to just 6 US cents today.

Despite economic stagnation, the South African capitalist class has retained its wealth, with the JSE share index soaring from 20,000 in 2009 to 85,000 today. The concentration of wealth at the top has become even more acute, with the richest 10 percent owning 86 percent of total wealth, while the top 0.01 percent hold more than the bottom 90 percent of the population.[34]

The apartheid regime and its capitalist support base were notoriously corrupt. Little has changed. Based on its biennial global survey of economic crime, Price Waterhouse Coopers consistently rates corporate South Africa as the "world leader in economic crime, including money-laundering, bribery and corruption, procurement fraud, asset misappropriation, accounting fraud, and cybercrime".[35]

The working class and poor

If the capitalists have fared reasonably well, the working class and poor have not. The country's Bill of Rights guarantees the right to health care, food, water, social security, education and adequate housing. What is the reality?

Unemployment now stands at 33 percent (43 percent if those who have given up looking are included), up from 25 percent in 2014. Sixty percent of 15-24-year-olds available to work are unemployed. Three-quarters of the unemployed have been out of work for a year or more.[36] Racial divisions persist: unemployment for whites is 9 percent, for Indians/Asians, 13 percent, for Coloureds, 23 percent, but for black people, 37 percent are jobless.

The main growth in jobs since 1994 has polarised between skilled and well-paid jobs in finance and business services and low-paid and low-skilled service jobs, such as security guards, care workers, domestic workers, office and hotel cleaners or construction labourers. Many such workers are without long-term contracts or benefits.

---

34. Chatterjee et al 2020.
35. Price Waterhouse Coopers 2018. The irony of PWC making judgements on economic crime should not be lost on readers.
36. Statistics South Africa 2024a.

The government's chief response to the unemployment crisis has been a public works program providing temporary work placements for the unemployed and a wage subsidy scheme encouraging bosses to take on young workers. The latter covered one million workers in 2015–16. This was a drop in the ocean compared to the eight million looking for work and is little more than a handout to employers.

In 1994, Cosatu was still a major force, reflected in the Constitution's Bill of Rights and the government's early labour laws, the Labour Relations Act of 1995 and the Basic Conditions of Employment Act of 1997. These laws governed workers' rights and gave unions greater power to negotiate collective agreements. In 1999, minimum wage laws were introduced for low-wage sectors with little union coverage, beginning with contract cleaners, domestic workers and farm workers and expanding to the wholesale and retail sector, private security and the taxi and hospitality industries. By 2007, these laws had grown to cover five million workers. In 2019, a national minimum wage of R20 per hour was introduced, a substantial increase on the sectoral rates it superseded, and covering nearly half of all workers

However, millions, including domestic workers, farmworkers and workers in the informal sector, lack the ability to enforce these rights. Forty-three percent of workers earn below the mandated minimum, 44 percent lack paid sick leave, and one-fifth work more hours than the legal weekly limit.[37] Despite wage improvements at the bottom, the dominant trend in the past 30 years has been the top 10 percent pulling ahead, squeezing the share of total income accounted for by the bottom half.[38]

The ANC government has implemented social programs to assist the poor, including home building and expanded access to water, electricity, education and health services. Household electricity access grew from 62 percent in 1994 to 87 percent in 2014, while piped water access increased from 4.5 million households in 2002 to 7.7 million in 2018. Over three million homes were built between 1994 and 2018. Financial support was extended, with monthly grants now covering half the population. A child support grant was introduced

---

37. Bhorat et al 2020, p.940.
38. Wittenberg 2017.

in 1998, and the Social Relief of Distress grant, launched as a temporary measure in 2020, has been made permanent. By the end of 2020, 23 million beneficiaries were receiving cash transfers, up from three million in 1995.[39] These measures have reduced absolute poverty and household hunger.[40]

Despite these measures, millions of black South Africans still live in poor conditions, with inadequate sanitation, healthcare and education, the quality of which is going backwards. About 2.2 million households, or 12.5 million people, live in informal settlements, shanty towns built on the outskirts of the cities and townships, with houses made of tin sheets and plastic tarpaulins. Rural areas, home to nearly half the country's children, face the worst conditions. Public services remain skewed toward the affluent, with well-funded schools in wealthy areas, while schools in poorer areas are underfunded, leading to high rates of illiteracy and innumeracy. The healthcare system is divided, with a comprehensive but costly private sector and an overburdened, inconsistent public sector.[41] The poor face higher rates of injury, mental illness, disease and mortality. Tuberculosis is widespread.[42]

South Africa produces and imports enough food to feed its population, but nearly a quarter of people live below the food poverty line.[43] Malnourishment affects a quarter of children under five, contributing to severe stunting. High unemployment, poor services and unhealthy diets contribute to obesity, with two-thirds of women and one-third of men being overweight, the highest rates in sub-Saharan Africa. Poor housing conditions put five to six million children at risk of gastrointestinal infections.

In the 1990s and 2000s, South Africa faced a severe HIV/AIDS epidemic, worsened by HIV denialism under Mbeki, which caused over 330,000 deaths from 1998 to 2008. While Mbeki's successor, Zuma, expanded access to antiretroviral drugs, AIDS still accounted for nearly 20 percent of deaths in 2017, especially among poor black South

---

39. May 2022.
40. Patel 2022.
41. Burger and Ngwenya 2022, p.850.
42. Burger and Ngwenya 2022, p.847.
43. Data in this paragraph are from May 2022.

Africans. Life expectancy for black South Africans remains about ten years lower than for whites.[44]

The government's financial assistance program covers half the population but is extremely stingy. Unemployment insurance covers just 60 percent of the labour force for a limited time. Most benefits are means-tested, reaching only those with the lowest incomes.[45] The median monthly wage for semi-skilled workers is R5,500 (A$470) and for elementary workers R3,500 (A$300), but the Social Relief of Distress Grant is only R370 (A$31). Monthly child support grants are R500 (A$42) but cut out for those earning more than R625 (A$53) a month. Many poor people rely on loan sharks to survive, with women facing the worst financial insecurity and high rates of domestic violence.

The expansion of social programs, cash transfers and installation of piped water and electricity have lifted living standards, but this has not significantly alleviated inequality of wealth or income since 1994, and inequality remains the most extreme in the developed world.

Although inequality between the races is lower now than in 1994, race is still a significant determinant of access to income, housing, public services, transport, schools, employment, safety and opportunities.[46] Median earnings for black people are 6 percent behind earnings for Coloureds, but 69 percent lower than Indians' and 78 percent lower than whites'.[47] Black people still suffer high levels of deprivation, and the spatial geography of apartheid remains – the deepest poverty and deprivation remain in the areas that were the Bantustans and townships under apartheid.

Foreign policy

Early in the ANC's period in power, Mandela stated that the government's "engagement in international affairs" would be guided by several core principles, including "the centrality of human rights, the

---

44. Burger and Ngwenya 2022, p.846.
45. Income data below are from Statistics South Africa 2024b.
46. Leibbrandt and Pabon 2022, p.179.
47. Statistics South Africa 2024b. These figures are not directly comparable with the 1994 data earlier in this article because they cover only earnings from employment, not total incomes. Income inequality is always more extreme than earnings inequality because it includes incomes from investments concentrated at the top end.

promotion of democracy and...the peaceful resolution of disputes between states".[48] Zuma claimed in 2017 that the ANC is the party of the "global anti-imperialist movement".[49] This rhetoric, however, is far removed from the government's practice, its submission to the ICJ concerning Israel's war crimes notwithstanding.

While South Africa does not follow the US blindly – for example, refusing to impose sanctions on Russia following its invasion of Ukraine – it nonetheless defends the Western imperialist world order. South Africa plays leadership roles in the World Trade Organization, the World Bank, the IMF, the World Economic Forum and the United Nations. It has hosted major forums of these bodies and, in Patrick Bond's account, remains "the continent's most dynamic site for elite networking".

Bond has described the ANC government's foreign policy as embodying "the dialectic of vague anti-imperialist rhetoric and concrete sub-imperialist practice".[50] This was obvious in 2003 when the US invaded Iraq, claiming it would bring freedom to the oppressed Iraqis. Mandela opposed the US invasion, saying: "If there is a country which has committed unspeakable atrocities, it is the United States of America". This had little effect on government policy, however. Within weeks, three Iraq-bound US warships had docked and refuelled in Durban, and South Africa's state-owned arms manufacturer Denel had sold $160 million worth of weapons systems to the British army and US Marines. A few months later, President Mbeki hosted a visit to Pretoria by US President George W Bush. In May 2004, Mandela phoned the US president to re-establish good relations, explaining: "The United States is the most powerful state in the world, and it is not good to remain in tension with the most powerful state".

The ANC government may oppose Israeli war crimes in Gaza, but it has joined the US and European powers in voting down attempts at the UN General Assembly to introduce reparations for slavery, colonialism and apartheid. It also rejects moves to cancel massive debts of the Global South owed to Western banks.

---

48. McKinley 2024.
49. Bond 2019a, p.83.
50. All quotes in this paragraph are from Bond 2019a.

As one of the biggest powers on the continent, South Africa continues to throw its weight around. It is home to one-half of Africa's largest firms, is the single biggest foreign investor, and has one of the most sophisticated militaries. It has used its economic and military clout to promote South African commercial and military interests and the broader US imperialist-dominated world system. This is apparent with the 15-member Southern African Development Community (SADC), the destination for most South African foreign investment. This free trade bloc is promoted as a means to stimulate mutually beneficial trade, investment and national development. However, as the most industrially advanced nation, South Africa benefits disproportionately from trade and investment liberalisation. It attracts resources from across the region, threatening the economies of its neighbours. Far from equalising the region's economies, SADC further deepens the core-periphery dynamic.

That South Africa might contribute to peace on the continent is also belied by its role as an arms exporter. It has sold hundreds of millions of rands worth of arms and armoured vehicles to conflict zones with human rights violations. The country also hosts the biennial Africa Aerospace and Defence Show, one of the largest arms fairs globally, attracting hundreds of defence companies.

South Africa's direct military interventions in Africa include a significant deployment to Lesotho in 1998, where 600 defence force personnel suppressed riots following a contested election, reinforcing South Africa's regional dominance and protecting mining interests. In 2007, it supported the authoritarian regime in the Central African Republic to safeguard mining investments. In 2013, South Africa joined UN peacekeeping in the eastern Democratic Republic of the Congo, where South African companies had extensive mining and oil interests, including a concession granted to a nephew of President Zuma. In 2021, responding to French requests, the ANC sent 1,500 troops to Mozambique to protect TotalEnergies' LNG facility from insurgency.

While promoting an "African Agenda," the government harshly treats irregular immigrants from neighbouring countries, conducting raids that result in mass deportations and allowing police harassment of migrants on the streets and in detention centres.

Working class resistance, repression and reaction[51]

The paradox of the democratic transition was that because mass action contributed to the establishment of democracy, the new ANC government came to power with more legitimacy than if it had emerged solely from high-level negotiations without pressure from below.[52] This did not mean, however, that its supporters were simply prepared to sit back and wait for the government to deliver.

The grinding poverty experienced by most black South Africans has fuelled decades of protest. Between 1997 and 2013, police records show an average of 5,000 protest events annually, with a steady increase from 2004 onwards.[53] There have been a range of targets. In the late 1990s, thousands of protests broke out in the townships opposing the introduction of user-pays water and electricity metering in poor areas and the subsequent water and power cut-offs for those unable to afford their bills.[54] Such protests have included boycotts, marches, submission of memoranda of grievances, mass community meetings, barricading roads, burning tyres, toyi-toying, street fights with the police, burning of municipal buildings and councillors' houses, and land occupations. These have compelled local municipalities, starting in 2001, to provide free basic services for low-income residents.

In the 1990s and early 2000s, the Treatment Action Campaign mobilised thousands of predominantly black women to demand generic anti-retroviral drugs when AIDS transmission was ripping through the black population. President Mbeki was eventually forced to provide the drugs. The outcome was a massive jump in life expectancy.

The Zuma presidency sparked years of protest against his administration and its corrupt relations with the Gupta faction of the state. Critical targets included the imposition of tolls on Gauteng freeways and the ongoing service delivery crisis. Zuma was eventually forced out.

In 2015, tens of thousands of university students demonstrated and occupied university buildings to protest against fee hikes. Activists also incorporated a demand that the outsourced and low-paid blue-collar

---

51. Thanks to Eddie Cottle for feedback on this section.
52. Ceruti 2021.
53. Bekker 2022.
54. Alexander et al 2018.

campus workforce be brought back in-house. The students and workers won, with the Zuma government first freezing fees and then introducing free tertiary education covering 90 percent of the student body. University administrations assumed responsibility for the grounds staff, cleaners, security staff, porters and hospitality workers.

Workers have struck and marched on the streets to press their demands, primarily for higher wages but also against privatisation, mass redundancies and hostile labour legislation. There have been several strike surges in the past couple of decades.[55] The first was in 2007, driven by the largest public service strike in South African history as ten unions with over 300,000 workers struck for 25 days. That year also saw several significant strikes in the rubber, metal and glass sectors, including the motor vehicle and engineering industries, and a spate of wildcat strikes in construction organised by independent worker committees. Foreshadowing the later upsurge in the sector, platinum miners also struck for 25 days. This wave of strikes helped shake up national politics, undermining Mbeki and paving the way for Zuma, who was regarded by Cosatu as more labour-friendly.

In 2010, with massive public spending underway leading up to the soccer World Cup, strikes peaked again, with 21 million strike days. Leading the way was a four-week strike by one million public sector workers, involving more than a dozen unions representing teachers, police, nurses, customs officials and office workers. Workers in publicly owned ports, pipelines, freight rail and passenger rail transport struck for and won big wage rises.

2012 saw two notable strikes. Platinum exports have become a major source of foreign exchange in recent decades, so when skilled rock drillers at Lonmin's mine at Marikana in North West Province struck for a R12,500 (A$1,066) monthly wage, substantially above the R7,000 median wage for the industry, and formed an independent workers' committee to run the strike, they drew national attention.[56] The issue at hand was not just the financial cost of lost production to the company and government but the threat the strike posed to the system

---

55. The following is from Cottle 2023.
56. The following account of Marikana and the reaction to the massacre is from Alexander et al 2012.

of industry-wide bargaining established in the 1990s. This corporatist system offered the NUM leadership and shaft stewards a privileged and well-remunerated role as representatives of mineworkers, in return for which they policed strikes. The wildcat strike by Marikana miners, some NUM members, others members of the new Association of Mineworkers and Construction Union (AMCU) that stood outside the Tripartite Alliance, threatened the NUM leaders' grip over the industry.

Management, the NUM and government ministers moved to smash the strike. The NUM denounced the strike and the workers' committee. Lonmin refused to meet with the Marikana workers' committee, stating that it would only negotiate with the NUM. Ramaphosa, at this stage a Lonmin director, urged the police minister to come down hard on the strikers and described the strike as "a criminal act". The stage was now set for a massacre. On 11 August, as mineworkers marched to the NUM office at the mine site to demand support, a line of 15–20 NUM leaders and shaft stewards fired at the workers, killing one. Several days of confrontation followed until, on 16 August, police and security forces, using armoured vehicles and helicopters, shot at a crowd of 3,000 mineworkers assembled at their strike camp, killing 34, many of them trying to flee.

Marikana was the bloodiest massacre by the state since Soweto, only this time, it was carried out with the blessing of the ANC government. In the aftermath, it was expected the mineworkers would return to work defeated. But they fought on, eventually forcing the company to concede substantial pay increases. The Marikana victory triggered a massive wave of unprotected strikes led by worker committees which spread from platinum mining into gold and onto other minerals.

The other notable strike of 2012 was a strike by farm workers in the Western Cape. In response to wage cuts by farmers used to ruling the workforce with an iron fist, a group of female seasonal workers struck to demand R4,500 per month. The strike then spread from farm to farm until it drew in 11,000 farm workers and encompassed 25 rural towns, becoming what Eddie Cottle calls "a social uprising of the rural working class".[57] The strike united permanent, casual and seasonal

---

57. Cottle 2023, p.118.

workers and was led by an informal organisation of farm workers, the first of its kind. Given its unprecedented nature, the strike garnered national headlines and forced the government to lift the official daily minimum wage for farm workers by 52 percent and, some time later, to extend minimum wages to a much wider section of the workforce, domestic workers included.

In 2014, platinum miners again came to the fore, with 70,000 mineworkers striking for five months, costing the platinum producers R24 billion in lost revenue. The miners eventually won a R1,000 monthly pay increase. The NUM, ANC and SACP again opposed the platinum miners. The platinum strike was followed by a four-week strike by NUMSA (National Union of Metalworkers) members in the steel and engineering sectors, with the workers extracting a big pay rise from the bosses.

The ANC government has done its best to dampen protests by offering community and student leaders grants and jobs in the ANC apparatus. They have been helped by the SACP and Cosatu, who have given the ANC government left cover. Since 1994, Cosatu has regularly registered opposition to the government's neoliberal measures or anti-labour legislation. It has organised national days of action with mass rallies in the big cities and repeatedly threatened to pull out of the Tripartite Alliance. However, the lure of jobs in the party and state apparatus and identification with the ANC's political project have prevented any schism (with an important exception we will deal with below). The NUM, in particular, Cosatu's largest affiliate, has been a conveyor belt for union leaders to progress to senior roles in provincial and national politics. The growth of public sector employment has bolstered the rolls and treasuries of the public sector unions, and these unions have been important government supporters.

While support for the government has yielded rewards for many union leaders, it has also helped hollow out grassroots union structures, a pale shadow of their state before 1994. Using the language of the national democratic revolution, the Congress Alliance helped steer the anti-apartheid struggle into reformist channels; the Tripartite Alliance plays this role today.

The growing gap between the official political structures and the working class helps explain the weakening of the hold of Cosatu and its constituent unions over the working class, evident in the emergence of independent worker organisations already touched on. These have sprung up in response to immediate needs when existing unions have not responded. However, in most cases, these have not survived long past the strikes they were set up to lead.

Cosatu has also experienced a major split. In 2014, the federation expelled the 350,000-strong NUMSA for refusing to back the ANC at the 2014 national elections. In 2017, NUMSA and a few smaller unions launched a rival federation, the South African Federation of Trade Unions (SAFTU). However, SAFTU has not pulled out any other big unions from Cosatu's ranks and is very much dominated by NUMSA. It is also wracked by faction-fighting, limiting its effectiveness. In 2018, NUMSA announced the formation of a Socialist Revolutionary Workers Party (SRWP) to challenge the ANC at the 2019 national election. However, the SRWP was a top-down initiative, reflecting a persistent Stalinist political outlook in the NUMSA leadership, and NUMSA failed to build it. The SRWP received fewer than 25,000 votes (0.1 percent of votes cast) in the 2019 election and soon after was quietly disbanded.

Another feature of class struggle in South Africa is the high incidence of unprotected strikes, where the workers or unions have not followed the official industrial relations procedures. In the past five years, between one-half and two-thirds of strikes have been unprotected, leading employers to bemoan the "lawlessness" of South African workers.[58] The attempt to pacify the working class by channelling disputes through the industrial relations machinery has only been partially successful.

Concessions and cooption have not been the ANC's only responses to mass protest. The ANC has also regularly denounced protests, sometimes referring to them as the work of foreign intelligence agencies collaborating with white intellectuals and opposition parties to destabilise South Africa's democracy. State security bodies regularly gather electronic and human intelligence on activists and groups planning protests. Local councils routinely misuse their powers to

---

58. Department of Employment and Labour 2024.

obstruct protests, framing them as a threat to public order, and then deploy police against those who assemble. And, as Marikana demonstrated, police attacks on worker and community mobilisations have resulted in fatalities.[59]

The social struggles that repeatedly break out in South Africa have their limits. Many are short and limited in scope, disappearing once the immediate issues of municipal corruption, service delivery failure, incompetent administrators or lack of consultation are addressed. Some result from turf wars between prominent individuals with fiefdoms to protect and who use struggles to bid for more funding, whether government or NGOs. There is little cross-fertilisation of community and labour struggles. Protests led by non-governmental organisations (NGOs) suffer the usual problems associated with this model: the dominance of professional organisers who steer the campaigns towards elite lobbying, the single-minded focus on the specific grievance and locality and the lack of interest in generalising the struggle.[60]

The situation is pregnant not just with the possibility of radical resistance but also of political reaction. Xenophobia is a running sore. Right-wing forces have seized on anger at housing shortages, lack of jobs, poor local facilities or overcrowding to attack immigrants, including shopkeepers and street hawkers from elsewhere in Africa or from South Asia. In 2008, repeated xenophobic attacks over several weeks left at least 64 dead and 70,000 people displaced in Johannesburg and Cape Town. In 2015, racist violence, which started in KwaZulu-Natal, erupted nationwide, resulting in at least seven deaths and displacing about 5,000 migrants and refugees. In 2019, the country experienced another wave of attacks against African foreign nationals.[61]

Anger and frustration have also been turned against informal settlements set up by impoverished rural migrants on the fringes of townships, with mobs destroying their makeshift homes. Ethnic divisions and reactionary moral codes are being promoted by traditional leaders working with the ANC's blessing. The ANC once

---

59. Duncan 2021.
60. Bond 2019b, pp.223–24.
61. Bond 2019a, p.89–90.

condemned many of them as apartheid collaborators, but as part of the negotiation compromises, agreed to preserve many of their privileges in the country's new constitution. These leaders have done their best to stoke ethnic and clan divisions to secure their authority. Ethnic identity has been used to promote reactionary attitudes towards women, LGBTI people and migrants, as have conservative evangelical churches which are drawing big followings in the townships and rural areas.

In 2021, Zuma's supporters triggered days of rioting and looting in Gauteng and KwaZulu-Natal following the Constitutional Court's decision to jail Zuma for 15 months for contempt of court after refusing to appear before the Zondo Commission of Inquiry into Allegations of State Capture that Zuma had set up in the dying days of his presidency. The 2021 riots were the most widespread and bloodiest example of disorder yet, resulting in more than 350 deaths. They also illustrated two sides of the current situation – the deadly factionalism within the ANC and the potential for revolt grounded in the widespread poverty of the masses.

Political consequences

Pessimism is pervasive in South Africa today. The sense that the country is "going in the wrong direction" is almost universal.[62] Two-thirds of the population are dissatisfied with the way democracy works. Nearly three-quarters think that the country's economic condition is bad and getting worse. Almost one-half say the same about their living conditions. Unsurprisingly, dissatisfaction with the state of things is significantly higher among those in poverty and those with little formal education. While the media focuses on crime, two-thirds or more of the population believe that unemployment is the country's most important problem, followed at some distance by electricity cuts, corruption, the cost of living and poverty. Ninety percent think that the government is failing to manage the economy successfully, whether that is keeping prices stable, creating jobs or narrowing income gaps.

The 2024 election showed that the ANC has seriously undermined its popular support. This was most obvious in the townships where the

---

62. The following data is from Hofmeyr 2024; Mpani and Ndoma 2024.

ANC once regularly recorded a vote of 90 percent or more. In Soweto and Tembisa, outside Johannesburg, and Khayelitsha on the dusty and impoverished Cape Flats, the party's vote share dropped to 50 percent. In Umlazi, a township of 400,000 on the outskirts of Durban, the ANC vote plummeted to just 13 percent. The ANC's falling vote share does not fully capture the drubbing suffered by the governing party since millions of registered voters stayed away from the polling booths and millions more, particularly young South Africans disillusioned with what was on offer, did not register to vote. Just 6.5 million out of an eligible voting age population of 42 million voted for the ANC in the 2024 election, down from 10 million in 2019, despite the population having grown by three million.

The ANC's electoral support is dwindling, but it is not about to collapse. It retains the support of the capitalist class insofar as it is the only party able to govern the country. Even now, it retains credibility with the black population in a way that the Democratic Alliance does not. The ANC, therefore, is more effective in suppressing working-class struggle than the DA. The ANC can also rely on the loyalty of the extensive party-state bourgeoisie it has built up over three decades, which owes its privileges to the ANC's continued hold on power.

If the ANC is no champion for the working class, this is also true of its rivals for the black vote. The biggest beneficiary of the ANC's falling support at the election was the uMkhonto we Sizwe (MK) Party, led by Zuma and launched only weeks before. MK very quickly drew to its ranks entire branches of the ANC apparatus in KwaZulu-Natal, Zuma's regional stronghold. It used this machinery to win 4.6 million votes (14.6 percent), only narrowly falling short of winning a majority in the province. This was the most dramatic electoral breakthrough for any party since the advent of democracy. The EFF, who had hoped to capitalise on falling ANC support, lost votes to MK but still scored 9.5 percent of the total. The IFP reversed its long-term decline since the 1990s, winning 3.9 percent of the national vote but 16 percent in KwaZulu-Natal. The Patriotic Alliance won 680,000 votes, only 2.1

percent of the national tally, but received 18 percent in voting districts dominated by Coloured voters.[63]

None of these parties has anything to offer the black and Coloured working class. The MK Party is a right-wing populist organisation combining demands for the expropriation of land without compensation and nationalisation of the mines, banks and insurance companies with Zulu chauvinism and support for an upper house comprising kings, queens and other traditional leaders. It is backed by conservative evangelical churches because it attacks LGBTI and women's rights in the name of upholding "African moral values" and supports compulsory military service to cultivate discipline and patriotism. It is essentially Zuma's faction of the ANC in exile, comprising those, gangsters included, who had benefited from his RET agenda while president and now impatient to get their snouts back in the trough. The Patriotic Alliance is also far-right and runs on a reactionary social program aimed at the Coloured population. The IFP leadership promotes the party as the voice of the KwaZulu-Natal "traditional leadership". The strong votes recorded for these parties show the dangers facing the South African working class when there is no significant left-wing political alternative to fight for working-class interests.

The EFF pitches itself as a party of the left. It was founded in 2013 by former ANC Youth League leader Julius Malema, who had been expelled the previous year. It draws support from young black people angry about the ANC's failure to lift the lot of so many poor South Africans and championed the cause of the Marikana miners. At the 2014 national election, the EFF picked up over one million votes (6.4 percent). In the 2019 election, it fared even better as frustration with the ANC grew, scoring nearly two million votes (10.8 percent). It has pushed aside the ANC to win control of student unions at ten higher education institutions. The EFF describes itself as "Marxist-Leninist" and African nationalist, identifying the radical intellectual Frantz Fanon and former Burkina Faso president Thomas Sankara as its ideological inspirations. Like MK, the EFF demands the expropriation and redistribution of land,

---

63. Scholz 2024.

the nationalisation of the big mining companies and the banks, and also a doubling of social payments and the minimum wage.

While describing itself as leftist, the EFF has no orientation to working-class politics. It backs strikes but does not build trade unions or working-class organisations of any kind. It supports Vladimir Putin and Russia's invasion of Ukraine. It also supports the Chinese Communist Party. Like all the parties represented in the parliament, the EFF leaders stand accused of financial corruption. It is run by a command structure on militaristic lines and is dominated by Malema. It has a mixed record on racism, at times opposing anti-immigrant racism and at other times vilifying Indian South Africans. And while it draws a vote from those angry at the lack of socio-economic progress since the fall of apartheid, it has, like the ANC, formed parliamentary blocs in municipal government with the Democratic Alliance. Having failed to form a coalition government with the ANC after the 2024 election, it has now joined MK in an oppositional Progressive Caucus, united by their mutual commitment to RET. While it is not fascist, as many South African liberals and the SACP describe it, it is in no way a socialist party and will be an obstacle if such is to be built.

Conclusion

The ANC and SACP have betrayed the hopes and aspirations of the millions of black South Africans who fought for decades to bring down apartheid. The Stalinist strategy of the two-stage revolution was a cynical cover for the Congress Alliance's actual project, which was to bring a new black ruling class to power. That has been achieved, but this has done nothing to transform the situation for the working class. The black ruling class superintends a capitalist system marked by continuities with that which existed before 1994. The bulk of property still lies in the hands of a wealthy minority, mostly still white, with whom the black ruling class shares the spoils of exploitation of land and labour of the mass of South Africans.

As guardians of the state apparatus, the black ruling class now stands in opposition to the black working class in the same way as its Afrikaner and British predecessors. It is black-run courts, black police and security ministers, black generals and police commissioners and often black bosses, all backed by black-run media, that confront workers in struggle today.

The fate of the South African struggle to smash apartheid has an important lesson for us today. Stalinism steered the South African struggle into a dead end. Unless capitalism is overthrown, the same evils will continue. Revolutionaries need to create a new socialist current, one that builds on the authentic Marxist tradition before Stalinism sabotaged it. A tough road lies ahead, but a start must be made. Crucial to the success of a revival of socialism in South Africa is a strategy that puts the fight for socialism at the forefront, not as some distant "second stage" of revolution. Our contribution to this project in Australia is to build the forces for socialism where we are. A revival of genuine socialist politics and organisation, wherever it takes place, can inspire the South African working class to again take up the fight for real liberation.

References

Alexander, Peter, Thapelo Lekgowa, Botsang Mmope, Luke Sinwell and Bongani Xezwi 2012, *Marikana: A view from the mountain and a case to answer*, Jacana.

Alexander, P, C Runciman, T Ngwane, B Moloto, K Mokgele, and N Van Staden 2018, "Frequency and Turmoil: South Africa's Community Protests 2005–2017", *South African Crime Quarterly*, 63.

Bekker, Martin 2022, "Language of the unheard: police-recorded protests in South Africa, 1997–2013", *Review of African Political Economy*, 49 (172).

Bhorat, Haroon, Ben Stanwix and Amy Thornton 2020, "Measuring multi-dimensional labour law violation with an application to South Africa", *British Journal of Industrial Relations*. https://doi.org/10.1111/bjir.12580

Bond, Patrick 2019a, "South African foreign policy and global governance: conflict from above and below", in Babalwa Magoqwana et al (eds), *Governance and the Postcolony: Views from Africa*, Wits University Press.

Bond, Patrick 2019b, "Neoliberalism, state repression and the rise of social protest in Africa", in B Berberoglu (ed.), *The Palgrave Handbook of Social Movements, Revolution and Social Transformation*.

Bredenkamp, Caryn, Ronelle Burger, Alyssa Jourdan and Eddy Van Doorslaer 2021, "Changing Inequalities in Health-Adjusted Life Expectancy by Income and Race in South Africa", *Health Systems & Reform*, Volume 7, 2021.

Burger, Ronelle and Mosima Ngwenya 2022, "The Economics of Health in South Africa", in Oqubay et al.

Ceruti, Claire 2021, "The end of apartheid in South Africa", in Colin Barker, Gareth Dale and Neil Davidson (eds), *Revolutionary Rehearsals in the Neoliberal Age: 1989–2019*, Haymarket Books.

Chatterjee, Aroop, Léo Czajka and Amory Gethi 2020, "Estimating the distribution of household wealth in South Africa", WIDER Working Paper, No. 2020/45, The United Nations University World Institute for Development Economics Research (UNU-WIDER), Helsinki. https://doi.org/10.35188/UNU-WIDER/2020/802-3

Cottle, Eddie 2023, "Industrial action in South Africa (2000–2020): Reading strike statistics qualitatively", *Global Labour Journal*, 14 (2).

Cowell, Alan 1985, "South Africans and top rebels meet in Zambia", *New York Times*, 14 September. https://www.nytimes.com/1985/09/14/world/south-africans-and-top-rebels-meet-in-zambia.html

Department of Employment and Labour 2024, *Industrial Action Report 2023*, Pretoria.

Duncan, Jane 2021, "A close look at how the net has tightened on the right to protest in South Africa", *The Conversation*, 12 March 2021. https://theconversation.com/a-close-look-at-how-the-net-has-tightened-on-the-right-to-protest-in-south-africa-156966

Hirsch, Alan, Brian Levy and Musa Nxele 2022, "Politics and economic policy-making in South Africa since 1994", in Oqubay et al.

Hofmeyr, Jan 2024, "Findings from the Afrobarometer South Africa pre-election telephone survey", 22 May, https://www.afrobarometer.org/wp-content/uploads/2024/05/SA-pre-election-survey-excel-23May24.pdf

Leibbrandt, Murray and Fabio Andrés Díaz Pabón 2022, "Inequality in South Africa", in Oqubay et al.

Makgetla, Neva Seidman 2022, "Mining and Minerals in South Africa", in Oqubay et al.

Mandela, Nelson 1956, "Freedom in our Lifetime", 30 June. https://sahistory.org.za/archive/freedom-our-lifetime-nelson-mandela

May, Julian 2022, "Food Security, Hunger, and Stunting in South Africa", in Oqubay et al.

McKinley, Dale 1997, *The ANC and the Liberation Struggle: A critical political biography*, Pluto.

McKinley, Dale 2024, "Unlike the government, we must practise what we preach", *Mail and Guardian*, 26 May. https://mg.co.za/thought-leader/opinion/2024-03-21-unlike-the-government-we-must-practise-what-we-preach/

Mpani, Nyasha and Stephen Ndoma, 2024, "South Africans score their government poorly on its economic performance", Afrobarometer Dispatch No. 816, 21 June. www.afrobarometer.org/publication/ad816-south-africans-score-their-government-poorly-on-its-economic-performance/

Ndletyana, Mcebisi 2024, "The Black Middle Class in the 2024 Elections: Signals from Johannesburg" in Collette Schulz-Herzenberg and Roger Southall (eds), *Election 2024: South Africa Countdown to Coalition*, Jacana Media.

Oqubay, Arkebe, Fiona Tregenna and Imraan Valodia (eds), *The Oxford Handbook of the South African Economy*, Oxford University Press.

Patel, Leila 2022, "Social Security and Social Development in South Africa", in Oqubay et al.

Price Waterhouse Coopers 2018, "Reported economic crime in South Africa hits record levels", 27 February. https://pricewaterhousecoopers-pwc.africa-newsroom.com/press/reported-economic-crime-in-south-africa-hits-record-levels-cost-and-accountability-concerns-rising?lang=en

Scholz, Dowie 2024, "2024 political earthquake: How shock results upended SA's electoral landscape", *News24.com*, 7 June. https://www.news24.com/news24/opinions/fridaybriefing/dawie-scholtz-2024-political-earthquake-how-shock-results-upended-sas-electoral-landscape-20240606

Southall, Roger 2014, "The black middle class and democracy in South Africa", *Journal of Modern African Studies*, 52 (4).

Southall, Roger 2023, "The middle classes and suburbia: desegregation towards non-racialism in South Africa?", *Journal of Contemporary African Studies*, 41 (1).

Statistics South Africa 2024a, *Quarterly Labour Force Survey, 2nd quarter 2024*. https://www.statssa.gov.za/publications/P0211/Presentation%20QLFS%20Q2%202024.pdf

Statistics South Africa 2024b, *Monthly Earnings in South Africa, 2017–2022*. https://www.statssa.gov.za/publications/02-11-20/02-11-202022.pdf

Tangri, Roger and Roger Southall 2008, "The politics of black economic empowerment in South Africa", *Journal of Southern African Studies*, 34 (3).

Vilakazi, Thando 2022, "Black economic empowerment in South Africa", in Oqubay et al.

Wittenberg, Martin 2017, "Wages and wage inequality in South Africa 1994–2011: Part 2 – inequality measurement and trends", *South African Journal of Economics*, 85 (2), June.

APRIL HOLCOMBE

Let a hundred flowers wither: the many failures of Western Maoism

April Holcombe is a long-term socialist and activist living in Sydney.

Introduction

THE 1960S AND '70s was the last time in Western countries that mass revolt radicalised an entire generation of youth. Student battles with police sparked a general strike in France in 1968; the US civil rights movement gave way to Malcolm X, ghetto uprisings and the Black Panthers; the 1969 Clarrie O'Shea general strike across Australia unleashed a rebellious spirit among rank-and-file workers for years to come.

The barbarity of America's war in Vietnam, and the international movement against it, was the central focus, especially after the turning point of the 1968 Tet Offensive, when the Vietnamese people launched an heroic surprise attack on the US.

At these various high points, and many others, tens of thousands of young people in the West became revolutionaries almost overnight. For a significant number of them, this meant becoming a Maoist.

Liberals and ex-radicals look back on this period with a mix of bemusement and horror. The peace-and-love "good '60s" gave way to the "bad '60s" – when angry young people wanted to "smash" things such as racism, capitalism and imperialism.[1]

This article regards the 1960s going "bad" extremely positively. Young radicals, no longer satisfied with registering moral opposition to war or racism, became much more serious and determined to put an end to the horrors of Western capitalism. In their impatient rage, their irrepressible defiance, and their sense of standing on the cusp of history, Maoism was one theory that could appeal.

In his history of the rise and fall of the US "New Communist" (Maoist) movement, former leading US Maoist Max Elbaum explains the attraction:

> The Communist Party of China (CPC) put itself forward as a new centre for the world revolutionary movement and promoted itself as the shining example and prime champion of liberation movements waged by peoples of colour all over the world... Western establishment ideologues promoted a mirror image of the Chinese argument, painting China as the most dangerous advocate of revolution on the planet.[2]

What did it mean to be a Maoist in the West? In China, the Communist Party had militarily conquered power in 1949 with a mass peasant army. It unified a long-fragmented territory under a centralised national state, defeating feudal landlords, corrupt Nationalists, and Western and Japanese imperialist plunderers.

How this experience – and later, the 1966 Cultural Revolution – could translate into conditions of advanced Western capitalism was contentious. Different Maoists had very different answers. "Western Maoism" therefore covered a wide range of overlapping, even contradictory strategies. Maoist groups could be authoritarian, conspiratorial sects or flamboyant, militant streetfighters – or both. Some advocated

---

1. For the quintessential ex-radical *mea culpa*, see Todd Gitlin's *The Sixties: Years of Hope, Days of Rage* (1987). Julia Lovell's recent liberal pop-encyclopaedia *Maoism: A Global History* (2018), similarly implies that a kind of violence-loving madness descended on Western youth in the late '60s.
2. Elbaum 2002, p.46. When read critically, Elbaum's is the most useful book written on US Maoism, or what he terms "Third World Marxism".

armed struggle from the slums and called Western workers "a parasite upon the heritage of mankind".[3] Others did the opposite, sending members into factories to become proletarian and get away from "petty-bourgeois" students.

The spectrum also ranged from "hard" Maoism, which closely followed the line from Beijing, to "soft" Maoism, which drew more diffuse inspiration from Third World, guerrilla and spontaneous youth rebellions. Examples of the latter include the very important workers' parties Avanguardia Operaia and Lotta Continua that came to prominence in the Italian Hot Autumn of 1969–70.

The primary focus of this article, however, will be on "hard" Maoism in three countries: France, the United States, and Australia.

By 1970, Maoism (often called Marxism-Leninism, and sometimes Third World Marxism) was, in many Western cities, the most influential organised force in the radicalisation. The Black Panthers, who sold Mao's Little Red Book on US street corners, toured China as distinguished guests. When the French government banned Maoist group La Gauche Prolétarienne, the world's most famous living philosopher Jean-Paul Sartre became their newspaper's editor and sold it on the streets of Paris.

Yet by 1980, Maoism in the West had all but evaporated. What happened?

From their formation in the early 1960s, Maoist groups posed as a radical alternative to the traditional Communist parties. Communists faced McCarthyite repression and still attracted militant unionists to their ranks. Since the 1930s, however, they had been marching into the political mainstream: supporting Allied governments in World War II, opposing strikes as undermining the war effort and rallying around the national flag. By the 1960s, Communists were tailing liberal pacifists (the US), running unions as bureaucratic machines (Australia and France) and even supporting colonialism (France).

By contrast, Maoist groups could appear bold, confrontational and activist. Maoists broke the US travel ban on Cuba, stormed the US embassy in Paris to hoist the North Vietnamese flag, and were

---

3. Cleaver 1969, p.8.

among those university students who scandalised Australian society by fundraising for the National Liberation Front. The New Left cried: "Victory to the NLF!"; the Old Left pleaded: "Stop the Bombings: Negotiate".

Maoists helped popularise the notion of Vietnam as an "imperialist" war. America was not making a moral mistake, but carrying out its ruling class's capitalist interests no matter the cost to humanity. For many young radicals, this represented a more systematic understanding of why the war was happening, and what it would take to end it.

Yet Maoism arguably turned out to be the most destructive and corrosive tendency of the new Western left. Although it spoke in abstractly Marxist terms about proletarian revolution and vanguard party-building, beneath the rhetoric lay an opposite world view: one of nationalist states, militarised struggle, authoritarian dictatorships and class collaboration. In this article, we will explore many problems with Western Maoism, but the underlying one is relatively straightforward: "Communist" China was simply another Stalinist police state run by self-interested, exploiting bureaucrats.

In a few short years, Maoist organisations chewed up and spat out thousands of courageous and committed activists. Western Maoism robbed a generation of its chance to rebuild mass movements for genuine socialism: internationalist, democratic, working-class and revolutionary. Then it imploded.

This article will begin by exploring the Stalinist origins of Western Maoism. It will then identify common "themes" in its theory and practice, although it should be noted that none of these are strictly universal. Over the course of its short life, Western Maoists drew their ideas and practice eclectically from high Stalinism, the Chinese Communist Party and other Third World struggles and regimes.

Stalinist origins

Despite appearances, Maoism was not an alternative to Stalinism. It began almost everywhere as an aggressive and self-conscious *revival* of Stalinism.

After Joseph Stalin died in 1953, the USSR disavowed his cult of personality and reign of mass murder. In a "Secret Speech" in 1956 the new USSR leader Khrushchev admitted to what Communist parties had always insisted were nothing but Trotskyite lies.

> [Stalin] used mass terror against the honest workers of the Party and of the Soviet state; against them were made lying, slanderous and absurd accusations... The confessions of guilt of many of those arrested and charged with enemy activity were gained with the help of cruel and inhuman tortures.[4]

The speech, published in the *New York Times*, sent shockwaves of disaffection around the world. Almost overnight, thousands left the Communist parties. Party leaders and apparatchiks abroad sought to suppress the speech entirely; internal discussion was squashed and dissenters expelled. When Russian tanks rolled into Budapest later that year to crush an anti-Stalinist revolution, Khrushchev used the same mass terror, cruel and inhuman tortures against revolutionary workers that he had denounced. More members left in its wake.

The Secret Speech marked a turning point in the consolidation of a new Stalinist orthodoxy. Concerned with stabilising its imperialist bloc in Eastern Europe, the USSR had begun arguing for "peaceful coexistence" with the West since the early 1950s, advocating for its Western satellite parties to openly pursue a gradualist, parliamentary road to socialism. Parties should allow more internal debate and engage in friendlier cooperation with right-wing social democrats such as the Australian Labor Party.

This provoked a sharp disagreement from the Chinese Communist Party (CCP). Fearing any thaw in US-Soviet relations would leave China out in the cold, CCP chairman Mao Zedong began criticising Khrushchev in increasingly bitter terms. This culminated in 1961 in an open breach, the Sino-Soviet split.

The CCP's polemics with the Communist Party of the Soviet Union (CPSU) looked like a dogmatic adherence to Marxist-Leninist orthodoxy. In a 1964 pamphlet, Mao Zedong harshly criticised Khrushchev as a "phoney communist" for calling the dictatorship of the proletariat

---

4. Khrushchev 1956.

no longer necessary in the USSR. Mao demolishes Khrushchev's substitute concept, the "state of the whole people", with quotations from Marx and Lenin. The pamphlet even cites reports of conditions in many Soviet enterprises. The corruption and self-enrichment of USSR bureaucrats in their despotic control over workers suggested that capitalism had been, or was being, restored. "The factories which have fallen into the clutches of such degenerates are socialist enterprises only in name, that in fact they have become capitalist enterprises by which these persons enrich themselves."[5]

The USSR and its satellite parties had become "revisionist", a favoured term of Maoism. The concept connoted a type of corruption of the ruling bureaucrats, who out of laziness, decadence or self-interest had turned their backs on world revolution. The CCP did not mince words:

> Khrushchev has been colluding with U.S. imperialism...opposing the revolutionary struggles of the oppressed peoples and nations, practising great-power chauvinism and national egoism… In completely negating Stalin, he has in fact negated Marxism-Leninism which was upheld by Stalin and opened the floodgates for the revisionist deluge…[6]

These polemics against "revisionism", however, were not about upholding a principled Marxism against the USSR. Instead, they were a self-serving smokescreen for the cynical conflict of interests between one state-capitalist regime and another. Firstly, there was the geopolitical competition typical between any nation states in world capitalism. Chinese and USSR spheres of influence overlapped in the Korean peninsula, Mongolia and Central Asia, where the much stronger USSR could obviously gain at China's expense. Secondly, the USSR's "peaceful coexistence" with the West included cancelling its former assistance with China's nuclear weapons program.

For China, a poor and encircled state-capitalist dictatorship, nuclear weapons were the fastest way to achieve geopolitical clout and national

---

5. Mao 1964.
6. Mao 1964.

"defence". The CCP's hyped-up rhetoric of imminent world war and revolution, as well as a cavalier attitude to the consequences of nuclear Armageddon,[7] were above all a justification to have the bomb. As the Chinese government complained quite openly in 1963: "If the Soviet leaders really practised proletarian internationalism, they would have no reason whatever for obstructing China from manufacturing nuclear weapons".[8]

Embattled and isolated, the CCP also had less to lose in its exaggerated calls for radical struggle and revolution across the world. In so doing, it hoped it might attract the allegiance of Communist parties in oppressed nations, and gain support among disaffected members in the West.

The Sino-Soviet split did indeed divide the Communist membership in countries such as Australia – but very unevenly.

> The vast majority of the Communist Party of Australia rank and file [were] anxious to find a way out of isolation after years of the Cold War... The extreme leftism of the Chinese rhetoric had no appeal to [those] who had spent the past decade learning to be restrained, moderate and above all devoted to a pacifist struggle against war.[9]

For some party apparatchiks, however, Mao was holding the line. They clung hard to Stalin-worship, monolithic leadership and hyper-denunciation. All they had ever known was how to obey, and command, absolute authority. China promised dogmatic purity and a new motherland. That is why early pro-China factions generally called themselves

---

7. "Launching a war using atomic and nuclear weapons, the result will only be the very speedy destruction of these monsters themselves encircled by the peoples of the world, and certainly not the so-called annihilation of mankind... On the debris of imperialism, the victorious people would create very swiftly a civilization thousands of times higher than the capitalist system and a truly beautiful future for themselves." From the editorial "Long Live Leninism" in the CCP central committee paper *Hongqi*, 8 April 1960, issue 8.
8. *Peking Review* 1953.
9. O'Lincoln 1985, p.105.

"Marxist-Leninists", after the state religion of the USSR expounded by Stalin, rather than "Maoists".

To genuine socialists, Stalin had long since butchered the revolution. Ample proof was provided in the form of gulags, purges, secret police, forced collectivisation, famine, ceaseless intensification of work, bureaucratic privilege, personality cults and the obliteration of democracy. As Leon Trotsky noted in 1937, "between Bolshevism and Stalinism [is drawn] not simply a bloody line but a whole river of blood".[10]

However, for the early Maoists, these atrocities were socialism's bread and butter.

The Communist Party of Australia's (CPA's) Ted Hill was a textbook case. A trade union lawyer, Hill served the party loyally for decades, both before and after Stalin's death. "To me words are not adequate to describe fully the grand picture of the new way of life in the Soviet Union", Hill wrote after attending the 1959 congress of the CPSU.[11] As Victorian state secretary, he had cracked down on dissent after the Secret Speech and according to fellow party leader John Sendy had his own factional spies.[12]

Hill could not countenance the partial loosening of internal party life that would take place in the ensuing years. After losing by 10 to 1 in the 1964 Victorian state conference election, he split to form the Communist Party of Australia (Marxist-Leninist), or CPA-ML. With him went a group of party functionaries and some popular trade union officials, including Victorian Tramways Union leader Clarrie O'Shea. For the next few years, the CPA-ML operated in absolute secrecy under the unquestioned authority of Ted Hill, who spent his time regurgitating reams of Stalinist dogma, making trips to see Mao, and contemplating a move to the Victorian mountains to train for guerrilla warfare.

The Stalinist origins of Maoism were similar in most Western countries. A failed election bid to the Communist Party of the USA's national committee saw long-term party organiser Milt Rosen establish

---

10. Trotsky 1937.
11. Hill 1959, p.1.
12. From Sendy's 1978 memoir *Comrades Come Rally*, cited in O'Lincoln 1985, pp.106–7.

a pro-China faction, arguing to go underground for the coming world war. Its expulsion in 1961 led to the founding of Progressive Labor (PL).[13]

Much the same split occurred in the adult French Communist Party (PCF) to form the PCFml. This was, however, overshadowed by a pro-China youth faction that formed in its student federation. These were avid disciples of the Stalinist philosopher Louis Althusser. After allying with their "revisionist" enemies in the PCF to drive out Trotskyist youth, they themselves were expelled and formed the Union of Communist Youth Marxist-Leninist, or UJCml, in 1966.[14] Its talented student leader Robert Linhart was toured through China by the Communist Party to witness the "Great Proletarian Cultural Revolution".

The numbers that broke away in these splits were initially tiny, numbering from a few dozen to a few hundred. However, they were flattered with official recognition from the CCP, the largest such party on the globe. China's predictions of imminent war, revolution and victory – not to mention its financial patronage – helped these tight, hierarchical, secretive organisations to persevere. Extreme grandiosity justified every form of thuggery against rival forces, and harsh internal suppression of debate. These practices already had long standing in the Stalinist movement from which they came.

Having established the Stalinist origins of Marxist-Leninist/Maoist splits, let us explore several recurring themes in their world view and practice.

Workerism

Most early Maoists were "workerist". They stereotyped workers, whom they sought to flatter, as socially conservative, and romanticised the image of working-class life. Hard labour was purifying, and workers were considered free from the bourgeois rot that infected all other individuals.

In France, thousands of UJCml students took Mao's advice to "come down from the horse to observe the flower" by going to the toughest

---

13. Morris Jr 1970.
14. Belden Fields 1988, chapter 3.

factories.[15] From 1967, student members were taken off the campuses, which were simmering with political radicalism, and sent to investigate or work in factories and on farms, which were not. This strategy was known as *établissement*.[16]

The students, who often had middle-class backgrounds, were anxious to purge themselves of it. Intra-group competition played a part here too. The older French Maoists of the PCFml, who although much smaller enjoyed official Beijing endorsement, touted themselves as the true proletarian group and relentlessly baited the student group as petty-bourgeois intellectuals.[17]

Beneath the anti-elitist pretentions of the Maoist dictum to "serve the people" lay a very elitist assumption. As with Stalin, Mao and their single-party dictatorships, Marxist-Leninists were the self-appointed vanguard on a messianic mission. One participant described the feeling for many of the students undergoing *établissement*:

> I wanted to put my head on the stock of the anvils, to disappear and be reborn, in another manner, in worker brutality... We venerated the people... We were strange shepherds who dreamed of being swallowed by our flock.[18]

Instead of building workers' *self*-confidence, the UJCml sought to win their passive *support*. The long-term strategy was to take leadership of the trade union confederation away from the PCF. There was little reflection on the class nature of the trade union bureaucracy; the problem stemmed only from the "revisionist" thinking that had infected its PCF leadership.

Établissement was a disaster by every metric. The students were muscled out by the Communist-controlled union machine, and worn out by the pace of work. In his own account, *L'établi* (*The Assembly Line*), Maoist leader Robert Linhart describes his self-imposed exhaustion:

---

15. Reid 2004.
16. See UJCml 1968.
17. Belden Fields 1988, pp.92–3.
18. Daniel Rondeau, *L'enthousiasme* (1988), quoted in Reid 2004.

> The first day in a factory terrifies everyone, many people will speak to me about it later, often with anguish. What mind, what body can accept this form of slavery, this destructive rhythm of the assembly line, without some show of resistance? It's against nature. The aggressive wear and tear of the assembly line is experienced violently by everyone, city workers and peasants, intellectual and manual workers, immigrants and Frenchman.[19]

Furthermore, workers were not the adoring chorus that so many had anticipated. The result was that hundreds of student activists quickly gave up on politics entirely.

Students were absolutely correct to see the working class as the agent of revolutionary change. But their energies would have been better served building pro-worker politics in the universities. Workerism, however, usually came with extreme hostility to any other social layer. So when students set up barricades and fought the police in the Latin Quarter of Paris, Linhart called it a "social-democratic plot, orchestrated by Trotskyists to usurp the working class's legitimate leadership of the struggle for the benefit of the petit bourgeoisie".[20]

This "social-democratic plot" was the famous May '68. It soon sparked the largest general strike in history. Events completely bypassed the Maoists' factory implantation. Instead, workers were radicalised by their visits to the Sorbonne university in May and June, where they intersected with many Trotskyist students. As one old militant at Renault recounted:

> Every evening I took five or six workers – quite often members of the Communist Party – in my car to the Sorbonne. When they returned to work the next day they were completely changed people… Many young workers rediscovered there in the Sorbonne the historic idea of the revolutionary traditions of the working

---

19. Linhart 1978, p.26. Linhart rejected some of the most extreme romanticising of the working class, and his characterisations in the book are frequently touching, humane and realistic. But this did not make the strategy any more successful for the organisation he led. Linhart suffered a nervous breakdown in the aftermath of the UJCml's colossal failure in 1968.
20. Quoted in Rekret et al 2022.

class, and started to talk the language of revolution... In the student demonstrations we were free to throw paving stones at the police. At the official trade union demonstration the main slogan was "Beware of provocateurs".[21]

The PCF and the unions infamously sabotaged the general strike, actions which both Maoists and Trotskyists rightly denounced. However, the PCF's betrayal was a repeat of its 1936 "Popular Front" government and their 1944 support for de Gaulle. These two policies had been laid down by the Maoists' hero Joseph Stalin.

Abstention from the central events of May 1968 provoked an internal crisis in the UJCml. They had built a reputation for street-fighting in the Vietnam War movement. Yet during the most significant Western upheaval since World War II, they completely failed the test. "In the demos of the first week of May much was expected of us from a military point of view. But we obviously brought nothing to it", Maoist leader Benny Lévy later admitted.[22] Convinced the problem lay in their incorrect reading of Marxist-Leninist dogma, most activists withdrew from all practical activity to study the holy texts. "It was a massive retreat. The UJCml was put to rest permanently."[23]

Social conservatism

The Maoists' workerism made them hardcore cultural conservatives in the midst of a blossoming counterculture. Members of Progressive Labor in the US, for example, had to be clean-shaven and neatly dressed, and were encouraged to marry. Marijuana use was strictly forbidden, since it was "pushed by the U.S. ruling class...to divert young people from struggling against them".[24] When they got work in factories to "serve the people", their jeans-wearing, long-haired, dope-smoking workmates thought they might be cops.

Stalin and Mao extolled "proletarian family values" because these ensured stable, self-reproducing units of exploitable labourers. All

---

21. Cliff & Birchall 1968.
22. Lévy 1971.
23. Belden Fields 1988, p.93.
24. Scheer 1975.

deviation was punished harshly. The Western Maoists transferred this line with gusto onto a generation of freewheeling youth. They generally dismissed women's liberation as "middle-class" and were, without exception, psychotically homophobic. By 1975, the largest US Maoist group was still proclaiming that "bourgeois society breeds and promotes homosexuality to degrade and enslave the masses of people, and it will be abolished".[25]

Sectarianism

The most hardline Maoists inherited from Stalinism the idea of a highly centralised, undemocratic party. They were extremely hostile to all others and could scarcely cope with being around them. Their dogmatic, brittle and authoritarian political culture suffocated debates. They pitted themselves against mass movements developing beyond their control, or producing new, more popular leaders. Even after launching worthwhile campaigns, they would beat an erratic, destructive retreat.

The experience of Progressive Labor in the US illustrates this perfectly. Through its strident pro-Black Power campaigning and a charismatic leader Bill Epton, the party enjoyed connections with Malcolm X's Organisation of Afro-American Unity. Their newspaper's front page became the unofficial poster of the 1964 Harlem riots. Epton, targeted as a riot ringleader, was the first person convicted of criminal anarchy since 1919.[26]

The next few years of rising Black struggle exposed PL to real-world, democratic impulses and inputs. PL's authoritarian leader Milt Rosen preferred to keep the group in what he called "glorious isolation". Epton's rising popularity had to be checked, and new West Coast chapters brought into line under the New York leadership. So when, in 1968, students of colour at San Francisco State launched the longest student strike in US history, demanding a Black studies department

---

25. *Programme and Constitution of the Revolutionary Communist Party USA*, 1975.
26. See Scheer 1975. If the history is even half accurate, PL began with quite an impressive first few years of activism, before utterly squandering it in the few years after that.

and more minority faculty, Rosen cracked down on the local PL chapter, which had initially supported the strike.

A new line was cynically imposed. The official PL position now called Black nationalism "objectively reactionary" and "counter-revolutionary". Since universities were capitalist brainwashing, more Black professors would merely be "changing the colour of the brain-washer's face", the party argued in a January 1969 issue of *Challenger*. When they presented their newspaper to student strikers, with its front page headline, "Don't support Black Studies!", any support for PL was instantly detonated. Dissenters inside PL were expelled in the aftermath.[27]

PL acted exactly the same way towards the anti-Vietnam War student marches they helped to initiate in 1964. From 1967, they abandoned the May 2 Movement on the basis that US imperialism was a "paper tiger" about to collapse anyway, and the North Vietnam government was "revisionist".[28] In reality, the movement had outgrown their petty control.

PL's next and most ambitious sectarian project was an aggressive takeover bid of the radical activist body Students for a Democratic Society (SDS). By 1969, SDS had 100,000 members nationwide, and was leading campus direct actions and mass demonstrations against the Vietnam War. Many SDS members were increasingly open to revolutionary politics. PL's goal was to "capture" SDS, have it adopt the PL program by hook or by crook, kick out whoever disagreed, and rule over whatever remained.[29]

The other student leaders of SDS were alarmed by the entrance of PL. Dogged, disciplined and drilled, PL members deployed endless denunciation and even physical violence against rival student activists. By contrast, most SDS veterans had fuzzy politics and only a few years' organising under their belts. Anxious to hold ground against PL, the SDS leadership began serving back the same hyped-up, denunciatory style. The ham-fisted dogma of Marxism-Leninism became the weapon

---

27. Dann and Dillon 1977, chapter three: "Retreat from the Black Liberation Movement".
28. Dann and Dillon 1977, chapter two: "The Retreat from the Anti-War Movement 1967–68".
29. For the definitive account of this saga, see Weinberg and Gerson 1969.

of choice for all sides. In the heat of a faction fight, the SDS leaders became, in the words of one Bill Ayers, who would soon form the terrorist Weatherman group, "the silliest, least intellectual group of Marxists ever".[30]

The SDS leadership exploited the most unpopular point of Progressive Labor's politics among radical students: its extreme hostility to Black nationalism. PL's magazine had described a 1969 Black Panther conference as a "circus of clowns and crackpots...true opportunists, racists and anti-communists...a sorry bag of accumulated scum".[31] The leaders of the Black Panthers were invited to the 1969 SDS national conference to drive PL out of the organisation.

The extremely bitter and hostile fight split SDS down the middle between the two factions. On one side were the workerist-Stalinists of Progressive Labor, the "first wave" Maoists. On the other were the Black Power-Student Power alliance of "second wave" Maoists. Within months, SDS was completely defunct.

Maoism had destroyed the largest, most radical student organisation in US history on the eve of a campus explosion. A few months later in 1970, four million students walked off campuses to protest Nixon's bombing campaign in Cambodia and the killing of four students at Kent State. The year after, public opinion polls showed three million people thought a revolution was necessary in the US. At this moment, an activist leadership, steeled by the struggles of the 1960s, was indispensable – but completely missing in action. "A nationwide student organisation...could have vastly strengthened radical initiatives during various 1969–72 upsurges."[32]

PL retreated into oblivion, selling its newspaper outside factory gates in rapidly diminishing quantities. The baton passed to the new, anti-PL student Maoists, who splintered into dozens of groups determined to build the one and only "vanguard party" on the immortal truths of Mao Zedong Thought. One quarter of the largest group immediately split off to train for guerrilla warfare in the San Francisco Bay Area. Most groups abandoned the campuses in favour

---

30. Quoted in Bailey 2003.
31. *Progressive Labor* 1969.
32. Elbaum 2002, p.73.

of "base-building" – this time in poor, Black and immigrant neighbourhoods. The Weather Underground became outright terrorists, blowing up government buildings and inviting government repression of the left.

More on sectarianism: Australia

As the 1960s progressed, some early Maoist groups began relaxing aspects of their workerism. In Australia, for example, the CPA-ML could see promising prospects on Australian campuses. They recruited the talented Albert Langer, a student leader in the Monash University Labor Club. Although the number of hardline Maoists never exceeded a dozen, they became the politically leading force in the club. With this leadership growing over campus politics, they would eventually establish the Worker-Student Alliance (WSA).

First initiated in January 1970 on the Monash and La Trobe university campuses, there were 14 WSA branches across Melbourne by November 1971, and 25 by February 1972. An estimated 1,000 to 2,000 high school and university students, workers and teachers were involved with WSAs at this high point.[33]

WSAs engaged in a variety of anti-war activism and local working-class community struggles. Connections to wharfies and construction labourers were facilitated by the CPA-ML, whose leaders controlled both the WSAs and a few blue-collar unions. This enabled some successful local campaigns such as preventing the eviction of public housing residents, and student-worker marches such as the Battle of Waterdale Road which defied police crackdowns.

Yet within a year or two, the WSAs were falling apart. The Maoists' sectarianism was catching up to them. They engaged in increasingly hyped up denunciation of their left-wing rivals, which ranged from decrying the "rubbish" and "filth" of campaigning around women's and gay liberation, to violent bashings of opponents, especially Trotskyists. One Trotskyist at LaTrobe was pushed through a plate-glass window by campus Maoists and required 50 stitches.[34] As we shall see later, other

---

33. Russell 1999, p.300.
34. "Maoist Thug Attack in Melbourne", *Workers' Vanguard*, 75, 29 August 1975, p.11.

components of Australian Maoist politics, namely their nationalism, would drive away whoever remained.

Through their control of several important trade unions, the Maoists used the same bureaucratic thuggery against workers. The leader of the Victorian branch of the Builders Labourers' Federation, the CPA-ML member Norm Gallagher, worked with construction bosses to smash up the NSW branch, which had been the most democratic, rank-and-file, radical and socially progressive union in Australian history.

The Cultural Revolution and idealism

A major component of both "hard" and "soft" Maoist appeal to students was the 1966 "Great Proletarian Cultural Revolution" in China. In reality a bureaucratic faction fight gone mad, it was sold as a radical youth revolt against tradition and authority. The Great Helmsman Mao Zedong was taking on those party bureaucrats threatening to restore capitalism in China with their "revisionist" thinking, and calling on students to rise up with him.

The entire conception of this "revolution", let alone its bloody reality, was a further degeneration from Marxism. If China was a classless communist society, why the outbreak of so much struggle and conflict? The Stalinist thinker Louis Althusser, a key influence on French Maoists, provided an answer. For Althusser, the Cultural Revolution proved that "class struggle can unfold in its purest form in the ideological sphere".[35] The classes of "class struggle" no longer had to exist in any real, material sense. Instead, "social classes are defined… depending on the side they take in political and ideological struggles". In other words: proletarians are those who think good, the bourgeoisie are those who think bad, and the Party, its great leader and its intellectuals, decide which is which.

Compare this idealism with the materialist principles laid out by Marx and Engels as early as 1845 in *The Holy Family*:

> It is not a question of what this or that proletarian, or even the whole proletariat, at the moment *regards* as its aim. It is a question

---

35. Althusser 1966.

of *what the proletariat is*, and what, in accordance with this *being*, it will historically be compelled to do. Its aim and historical action is visibly and irrevocably foreshadowed in its own life situation as well as in the whole organisation of bourgeois society today.[36]

Maoism was a regression to pre-Marx idealism. Proletarian was a state of mind, not an objective class position. Peasant armies, bands of guerrillas, tiny student groups or exploitative police dictatorships could all be proletarian – so long as they said so. The Stalinist and Maoist conception of the party was "almost a metaphysical entity into which the working class has been transubstantiated".[37] If such a party ruled society, then by definition that society was socialist, or on the way there.

Factional fights in the ruling strata of Stalinist dictatorships, and conflicts within the global "socialist" camp, were explained with the moralistic theory of revisionism. Revisionism was an eternal risk for any socialist society: at any time, its leaders' descent into "bourgeois thinking" could snowball into the full-blown restoration of a capitalist economy – all without the attention or activity of the masses. The party leadership then, was in an eternal war for the right line of march, requiring constant ideological purification.

Purity

Maoists therefore placed an extreme emphasis on individual purity and sacrifice. Psychological transformation, not real-world mass struggle, was crucial. Criticism-self-criticism circles were designed to ideologically "remould" individuals into the great leaders of tomorrow. These encouraged an inward-looking, therapeutic politics – similar to, and cross-fertilising with, the consciousness raising circles of women's liberation.[38] In turn, it paved the way for more contemporary lifestylism, call-out culture and checking one's privilege.

The grandiose, authoritarian style of these small groups often

---

36. Marx and Engels 1845, chapter four.
37. Weinberg and Gerson 1969, p.8.
38. For an example of the overlap in Australia, see Russell 1999 on male chauvinist self-criticism in the Maoist-led Worker-Student Alliances, pp.304–5.

allowed strange and abusive behaviour to flourish. Where such groups did not entirely descend into cults, they skirted dangerously along the perimeter. This has been a favourite trope of liberals ever since, to tar the entire far left with the same brush. Guru charlatans such as US Maoist leader Bob Avakian were proof that revolutionary politics and the Manson family existed somewhere on the same "bad '60s" bandwidth.

Dogma

Alongside personal purity went ideological purity. Maoists did not understand that mass movements and revolutions were expressions of deeper, objective processes. Instead, the most popular dictum of 1970s US Maoism was that "the correctness or incorrectness of the line determines everything".[39] This had disastrous consequences. Whenever struggles faced a setback, or groups failed to grow, an incorrect idea was entirely to blame. That meant the little vanguard party had been infiltrated by a "bourgeois headquarters" (such headquarters could be established among a dozen people). Debate became almost impossible to keep at the level of tactical difference. As struggles quickly declined through the 1970s, splits were frequent, traumatic, and strengthened cult of personality leadership styles.

The ideas that guided Maoists and "determined everything" were little more than comforting, self-assured, sterile, abstract dogma. The core text, *Quotations from Chairman Mao Zedong* or the "Little Red Book", ranges from the facile to the objectionable. Some examples include: "Be united, alert, earnest and lively"; "Serve the people, heart and soul"; "Combat liberalism"; "China's women are a vast reserve of labour power"; "The atom bomb looks terrible but in fact isn't"; "Hungary in 1956 was a case of reactionaries inside a socialist country, in league with the imperialists".[40]

The book, however, was enormously popular on the Western left. After its translation into Swedish in 1967, over 100,000 copies were sold in a population of 8 million.[41] But adherence to the book had more in

---

39. Elbaum 2002, p.238.
40. Mao 1966.
41. Johansson 2012, chapter 8.

common with religion than politics. So did the Mao caps, Mao suits and portraits of the "reddest, reddest red sun of our hearts Chairman Mao".[42]

Politics is tested by real-life struggle and vigorous debate. Theory is informed by studying history and political economy. The Maoists placed little importance on these. So Elbaum reflects that the Maoist left,

> in contrast to nearly every other 1970s/early 1980s US left tendency, issued almost nothing in the way of original studies illuminating new features of US social and economic development or hidden chapters of US history…almost nothing that remains of value to serious left researchers and scholars.[43]

Substitutionism

For Marxists, the proletariat is a unique social class. It alone has the power to replace the capitalists' control of the economy with a democratic, socialist society. The working class occupies the heart of our profit-making society and can bring it to a grinding halt. Workers labour and strike as a collective, and can only take control of production on the same basis, not as individual producers or property owners. And workers do not exploit or oppress anyone else in society. A revolution that brings democratic workers' councils to power will liberate all oppressed people.

Despite a lot of rhetoric, in practice the Maoists rejected this. Workers were not a unique class. Any layer that desired revolution could *substitute* for them so long as, through sheer brute force, it could establish the rule of a "Marxist-Leninist" party. Their vision of socialism, after all, included a peasant army led by intellectuals establishing a police state led by bureaucrats. This allowed immense ideological and strategic "flexibility" (and indeed "revision") for Maoists about

---

42. "Women xinzhong zuihong zuihongde hong taiyang Mao zhuxi", poster from the Cultural Revolution, 1968. https://chineseposters.net/posters/e3-712
43. Elbaum 2002, p.324.

who to build a "base" among. It could just as well be students, farmers, or in the slums.

As we have seen, Western Maoists spoke a lot about workers. However, this was never as agents of their own struggle and emancipation. They were advanced capitalism's equivalent of the Chinese peasantry, a standing army of support for elites to seize power on their behalf.

This explains the fact that despite their formal adherence to "orthodoxy", and despite their dizzying array of strategies and perspectives, one concept is universally absent from Western Maoism: workers' democratic councils. The beating heart of the Paris Commune, the Russian soviets and many other inspiring revolutions was torn out. In fact, Maoists sometimes explicitly ruled it out. In a 1969 polemic, the "anti-hierarchical" Gauche Prolétarienne dismissed French Trotskyism's call for workers' control of industry as reformist, arguing: "Revolutionary power...combines two essential conditions: the support of the masses and the gun".[44]

Voluntarism

As the 1960s and '70s wore on, the influence of Third World struggles tended to weaken workerist tendencies and strengthen voluntarist and nationalist tendencies in Western Maoism. These were the final nails in its coffin.

The belief that sheer willpower could transform society (voluntarism) was a widespread affliction in the 1960s. Life had become one demonstration after another and a heady feeling of momentum naturally emerged.

Third World resistance – from Fidel Castro and Che Guevara to Ho Chi Minh – seemed to prove that guerrilla brilliance and personal heroism could overcome even the strongest imperialist powers in the world. So-called "objective conditions" – state power, capitalist control of production, workers' passivity, division and alienation – could be defeated by subjective initiative alone.

Maoists were voluntarists par excellence. "A single spark can light

---

44. La Gauche Prolétarienne 1969a.

a prairie fire", the Little Red Book remarks. Ultra-militant confrontation would shock people into action and draw them behind Maoist leadership. Sometimes this proved effective, such as when Melbourne Maoists helped lead a riot outside the US consulate on 4 July 1969. Ruling class repression, it was argued, would then educate protesters on the true nature of the "fascist capitalist state". This was also sometimes vindicated, as when those same Maoists occupied Monash university buildings, leading to expulsions that angered and electrified the campus' entire student body.

However, at other times, the same actions alienated others, invited heavy repression, and left radicals isolated. Undoubtedly, if socialists are not to become passive and ineffectual, they need to take risks and act in the hope of inspiring broader resistance. Yet this must be done with real objective conditions in mind. Where actions fail or backfire, then retreat, regroupment and sober reflection are necessary. These in turn require robust internal cultures of democratic debate.

The Maoists, however, had only one gear, quickly becoming locked in cycles of confrontation-repression-confrontation. As one former CPA-ML member describes:

> The CPA-ML leadership and its youth wing spurred each other on, generating an inexorably leftward momentum. Armed struggle for the overthrow of capitalism was envisaged as growing out of the steady escalation of the level of violence at street demonstrations.[45]

In Australia, street battles and reprisals very quickly reduced the struggle to a minority of heroic individuals and mass of spectators. Each round of occupation at Monash University led to new disciplining of the Maoist students, who responded each time with smaller and less effective occupations.

The more difficult the objective circumstances, the more desperate and destructive became Maoist tactics. A deeper slump needed a more dramatic "spark" to shock it back to life. Since repression reinforced

---

45. Herouvim 1984.

feelings of weakness in the masses, and the left's isolation from them, Maoists were on a tactical death-spiral.

This took devastating hold in France after 1968. Reeling from their failure to connect with the May revolt, a new Maoist group emerged: La Gauche Prolétarienne (GP). Influenced by the mystique of the Cultural Revolution, GP valorised maximum, spontaneous, violent confrontation of any kind. Their flamboyant tactics brought them to infamy. In 1970, they "liberated" sacks of caviar, foie gras and champagne from a Paris luxury food store, and redistributed it to a poor French-Algerian neighbourhood. ("We're not thieves, we're Maoists", their leaflet explained.[46])

But their tactics had little to do with rebuilding a mass movement from the ground up after the defeat of 1968. GP wanted to immediately bypass the trade unions, which "we don't hide the fact that we are resolutely opposed to", they wrote in a 1969 document, *Blow for Blow*.[47] Raising any demands was reformist.

Factory militants connected to GP smashed up machines and bashed foremen and managers. This isolated radicals from their workmates and made them targets for repression. After the GP was banned by the government in 1970, they renamed themselves the ex-GP and increased confrontation. Worker member Pierre Overney was murdered in a fight with factory security in 1972. An enormous flood of sympathy followed from workers and the entire left, as 200,000 people attended Overney's funeral.

Yet the response of the ex-GP destroyed whatever could have been made of this moment. An ex-GP commando group kidnapped his boss, holding him hostage for two days before being forced to surrender him unconditionally. This not only destroyed the Maoists but led to extreme demoralisation on the Left. "It became virtually impossible to do political work at the Renault plant after this affair", wrote Belden Fields.[48]

Substituting themselves for the working class took its most extreme form in left-wing terrorism, which plagued West Germany, Italy and

---

46. Lovell 2015, p.315.
47. La Gauche Prolétarienne 1969b.
48. Belden Fields 1988, p.113.

Greece in the 1970s. Maoists, although not only Maoists, took part in this, irreparably damaging whatever links had been established between the far left and the workers' movement.

Third Worldism

Maoism at its core was for national struggle, not class struggle. The world was not divided between an international working class and the ruling classes of each national state. Instead, it was a fight between the "proletarian" China and allied Third World nations against the "bourgeois" United States and Western nations. People's Liberation Army leader Lin Biao called it "the principal contradiction in the contemporary world".[49]

However, while national liberation struggles were progressive, they were rarely socialist. Much more typically, they were led by intellectuals and army officers, and more likely to mobilise the peasantry or poor than the working class proper. Where they succeeded, they either set up capitalist democracies, such as India or Sri Lanka, or established flat-out dictatorships over the working class, as in Egypt, Ghana and Vietnam. The latter were frequently in the name of "Arab socialism", "pan-African socialism" or straight-up "Marxism-Leninism". Yet, ruled by a small elite, their interests remained the same as for any national state in the global capitalist system: competitive exploitation of the labouring population, as well as safeguarding and expanding influence and control over territory and resources.

Instead, Maoists considered certain Third World nation states as acting in selfless regard for world revolution. Since they saw the world as divided between good and bad nations, rather than exploited and exploiting classes, Maoism was a *nationalist* ideology. World revolution was never envisaged as an international working-class chain reaction that demolished all borders. It was, at absolute best, the accumulation of "Socialism in One Countries".

Where the Western workers' movement was weakest, in the United States, the nationalist bent of Maoism was strongest. In particular, Mao's China became a guiding star for many radical Black nationalists.

---

49. Lin Biao 1965, chapter 8.

They theorised themselves as an "internally colonised people", a separate Third World nation within the United States. The first Black Maoist organisation in the US, the Revolutionary Action Movement (RAM), established in 1962, conceived of their liberation completely in terms of Third World people's war. "What we got from Mao…was that the countryside or the peasantry of the world would move first and surround the cities of the world. We saw ourselves as the peasants surrounding the cities. Seasonally employed black men."[50]

These extraordinarily defiant activists had a burning hatred of the system, but lacked any coherent vision for how the economy and society might be transformed. The Fall 1964 issue of their magazine *Black America* described a liberation war taking about 90 days:

> Chaos will be everywhere… The revolution will "strike by night and spare none"… The Black Revolution will use sabotage in the cities, knocking out the electrical power first, then transportation and guerrilla warfare in the countryside in the South. With the cities powerless, the oppressor will be helpless.[51]

Apart from the implausibility of the oppressed Black minority alone overpowering the US state, there is no explanation for how a military uprising of itself would abolish capitalist relations of exploitation and replace them with collective, classless production.

RAM was a major ideological and organisational influence on the much more famous Black Panther Party. Both conceived of the revolution primarily in military terms. Whoever was most receptive to immediate violent action was the most radical class. For Panthers, this meant recruiting from the lumpenproletariat – gang members, petty criminals, "brothers on the block": people "who would rather punch a pig in the mouth and rob him than punch that same pig's time clock and work for him".[52]

---

50. Muhammad Ahmad (formerly Max Stanford), RAM founder interviewed in Lovell 2019, p.305. Lovell's book is a liberal mishmash and is not recommended reading.
51. Cited in Kelley and Esch 1999, p.17. This article is highly recommended for exploring the ideological precursors to the Black Panther Party.
52. Cleaver 1969, p.7.

The problems with the Black Panther revolution were tragically exposed from 1970. Their armed patrols and "serve the people" breakfast program inspired the oppressed ghettos to stand taller, yet this could not substitute for the powerful collectivity of organised workers. The Black Panther Party was quickly and savagely broken by a US government campaign of murder, repression and infiltration.

In their time the Black Panthers were, in turn, a major ideological influence on the broader, mostly white student movement. When they waded into SDS in 1969 (see above) and raked the "white, racist, counter-revolutionary" PL over the coals, hundreds of guilty white SDSers squirmed in their seats. In the crucible of Black Panther worship, liberal white guilt and anti-PL crusading, a new "flavour" of Maoism formed among radicalising students. Workerist Maoism was out, and Third World Maoism was in. It stressed the "white-skin privilege" of US workers that made them racist, pro-US imperialism and counter-revolutionary.

The moralist, elitist prejudices of many students carried over perfectly into this Maoist conversion. Western workers striking for higher wages was a selfish, dirty and irrelevant thing to the world revolution, since their "television set, car and wardrobe already belong, to a large degree, to the people of the rest of the world".[53] The Marxist notions that workers had shared interests across nations and racial and gender divisions, and that workers' struggle anywhere helped struggles of the oppressed everywhere, were rejected or downplayed.

Instead, the vast majority of the American working class were seen as useless, if not an active enemy. As economic beneficiaries of the US war machine, the revolution would be in spite of them, even against them. The defeat of the American ruling class would require a war of the Third World against the US, with Black people as an internal flank and white radicals as a self-flagellating cheer squad.

After the SDS explosion had produced a new generation of Third World Maoists, the national thesis was applied to every racially oppressed group in the US. Each "internally colonised people" had its own national struggle, so each organised separately. There were Black

---

53. Ayers et al 1969, p.2.

Maoist groups, Puerto Rican Maoist groups, Latino Maoist groups, Asian Maoist groups, and white Maoist groups. They rejected the view that racially oppressed workers formed sections of a broader US working class. That led them into a range of confusing positions: the Black-led Communist League argued in 1972 for a new independent state in the US South made up of both "Black Negroes" and "White Negroes".[54]

The confusion reached a low point in 1974 with the Boston "busing crisis". The plan was to bus Black children to white schools to help desegregate public education. Widespread, violent opposition from white racists galvanised Black community resistance in turn. Hoping to breathe new life into a considerably declined civil rights struggle and resist a burgeoning racist backlash, anti-racist activists mobilised en masse to Boston.

Yet more than one Maoist group, including the country's largest Revolutionary Union (RU), stridently *opposed* busing. They argued it was a form of racial dilution of the Black, Latino and Asian "nations". Others argued it was a "monopoly capitalists' plot" to stoke up racism within the white working class. Some made both claims!

Activists with RU arrived in Boston in October 1974 with their newspaper bearing the headline: "People Must Unite to Smash Boston Busing Plan!". From uncritically worshipping the Black Panthers, this white-majority Maoist group had come to a strange alignment with segregationists. As Elbaum recounts:

> The issue was published at the same time as the most aggressive advocates of smashing the busing plan were physically attacking Boston Blacks on sight – and more than one Bostonian thought on first glance that the RU publication was a right-wing tabloid.[55]

The RU's bitter split in the aftermath was by now standard fare.

---

54. Elbaum 2002, p.194.
55. Elbaum 2002, p.191.

Australian patriotism

From the late 1960s onwards, the CPA-ML applied this nationalist thesis to equally reactionary effect in Australia. The CPA-ML argued Australia was an oppressed nation like China or Vietnam, and would first need to win independence from US imperialism before any talk of socialism. The first-phase national struggle would not be led by the working class but by a broad coalition of all "patriotic" forces, what Mao had called the "bloc of four classes". How broad was this coalition? "We are even prepared to unite with some sections of the national bourgeoisie and internationally with other imperialists to form a united front of 90 percent of the world's people to defeat US imperialism", a 1971 WSA statement declared.[56]

Alongside their violent behaviour and sectarianism, this bizarre position drove out the remaining genuine progressives activists in the Worker-Student Alliance. The Maoists could now struggle uninhibitedly "for an independent Australia". They embarked on a "Long March" across regional Victoria, alerting farmers to the dangers of a Japanese invasion.[57] They initiated the Blinky Bill Brigade to campaign against the Yankee imperialist Mickey Mouse, who in 1977 had been crowned King of Moomba, a Melbourne cultural festival.[58] A member of the campaign entered the float dressed as Blinky Bill while another "dressed in a rat's costume and also went along to agitate and take the focus away from Mickey Mouse".[59] The road from the 1949 Battle of Chengdu to the 1977 Battle of Moomba was a long and tortuous one.

Chinese foreign policy

One of the most decisive blows to Western Maoism came from Mao himself. After meeting with US president Richard Nixon in 1972 and securing American "friendship" against the USSR, Mao exported a new line to the international Maoist movement. Soviet "social imperialism"

---

56. Cited in Russell 1999, p.308.
57. Russell, p.306.
58. Armstrong, p.105.
59. Campaign poster and account at *Art Workers Archive*, https://www.communityartworkers.com.au/mickey_moomba.php.

was now objectively the greater evil, and the United States might, in some cases, be a force for good.[60]

Implacable opposition to US imperialism had been the Maoist selling point. Now hardline Maoist groups sided with US- and apartheid South Africa-backed groups in Angola against popular national liberation forces. From uncritical supporters of national liberation movements, Maoists became opponents of independence for Bangladesh (as West Pakistan's military butchered millions) and for Puerto Rico (a colony of the United States). When the Portuguese revolution broke out in 1974, the most hardline Maoists sided with the NATO-aligned Socialist Party against the revolutionary left. In West Germany, some Maoist groups had gone over to supporting NATO outright, a move echoed by some US groups who called for more US bases in the Philippines.

Mao's China was one of just three countries to keep its embassy open in Augusto Pinochet's Chile from day one after its brutal coup against the Salvador Allende government, and the ensuing murder of thirty thousand leftist workers. Those groups most eager to maintain their official ties with Beijing (or to poach them from a rival) complied with China's silence over Chile.

The Khmer Rouge genocide in Cambodia, backed by the CCP, was a step too far for some. Yet the movement had trained plenty of yes-men willing to toe the line to the bitter end. After a 1977 tour of the country, Ted Hill wrote in *Vanguard* the following year: "The Communist Party of Kampuchea are building socialism. Their successes are inspiring... There is a great hooha about Phnom Penh being virtually without people... It is quite right that people should not eat unless they work".[61]

After the Khmer Rouge genocide, Vietnam invaded Cambodia, China invaded Vietnam, and the Soviet Union threatened to invade China. The entire "socialist" camp was falling apart. Some disoriented Maoists shifted their loyalties to Vietnam. Yet Vietnam was allied with the "revisionist" USSR; soon, it would join China in opening up to the free market, and later form a friendship with US imperialism.

---

60. See Elbaum 2002, chapter 10.
61. From the April 1978 issue of CPA-ML publication *Vanguard*, cited in Smith 1922.

Conclusion

Western Maoists had tied themselves up in knots, excusing the crimes and following the twisted lines of Third World ruling classes aligned with the CCP. Once the bonds broke, they flew off in every direction. Most of what was left of the US Maoists flooded into the capitalist Democratic Party to support the presidential nomination campaign of civil rights leader Jesse Jackson – a move that Elbaum lauds as a break from the sectarian, dogmatic past of the old Maoists (today, Elbaum supports voting for Kamala Harris)[62].

A disproportionate number of French Maoists became "New Philosophy" hardline advocates of neoliberalism. After his release from prison, GP leader Alain Geismar left to form a commune, and later returned to politics as a social-democratic government minister. Australian Maoists found their way into the Greens, into academia, into sectarian irrelevance.

But most tragically, the vast majority simply dropped out of left-wing politics. They equated socialism with their time in the Maoist movement and became bitterly disillusioned. Maoism was by no means the only politics guilty of workerism, sectarianism and the like: other tendencies also played a counterproductive or outright destructive role. However, Maoism took these faults to their extremes and applied them with a cynical ruthlessness worthy of its Stalinist inheritance.

The radicalised youth of the 1960s had the odds stacked against them. Their task was to build something entirely new after decades of Stalinist domination over the left. Then the mid-1970s downturn in workers' struggle and the triumph of neoliberalism condemned every left tendency to much tougher isolation than any had bargained for.

Nonetheless, if from the outset the dominant alternative to Stalinism had been genuine Marxism, then the 1960s could have been a major breakthrough for the Western working-class movement. Instead, Maoism – a rehashed Stalinism with organisational continuity from counter-revolutionary Communist Parties – got there first. "The bitter final legacy of Stalinism in Australia was the destruction of the

---

62. See, for example, Elbaum 2024, in which he argues for an "anti-MAGA front" united behind the Democratic Party to stop the fascist Trump.

best opportunity in thirty years to build a socialist party that could challenge the tepid reformism of the ALP".[63]

Despite starting from very small numbers, genuine anti-Stalinist Marxism grew in the 1960s and has survived until today. In particular, the International Socialists[64] from the beginning opposed Washington, Moscow, Beijing, social democracy and union bureaucracy. This tendency looked to the bottom-up international class struggle to change the world, kept to the spirit of Trotskyism and not always to the letter, and critically analysed new world politics and trends. Its endurance has provided a living link between the 1960s generation and activists today. This is a modest but important legacy. Without the destructive influence of Maoism, their numbers and influence might have been much greater.

As a new generation incipiently breaks with capitalism, and a minority thereof search for radical alternatives, there is some risk of Maoism – with its "romantic" mix of guerrilla chic, Stalinist kitsch, and revolutionary phraseology – experiencing a revival. The disaster of Maoism during the last major Western upsurge must not be forgotten, and must not be repeated. Instead, activists must prepare for the future by studying our past and organising around the politics of genuine Marxism.

References

Althusser, Louis 1966, "On the Cultural Revolution", *Cahiers Marxistes-Léninistes*, translated and re-published by Jason Smith in *Décalages* 1 (1), February 2010, pp.1–18. https://decalagesjournal.org/wp-content/uploads/2024/09/decalagesvol1iss1_ocr.pdf

Armstrong, Mick 2001, *1, 2, 3, what are we fighting for?: the Australian student movement from its origins to the 1970s*, Socialist Alternative.

Ayers, Bill, Bernardine Dohrne et al 1969, "You Don't Need A Weatherman to Know Which Way the Wind is Blowing", *New Left Notes*, 4 (22), 18 June. https://www.sds-1960s.org/NLN/NewLeftNotes-vol4-no22.pdf

Bailey, Geoff 2003, "The rise and fall of SDS", *International Socialist Review*, 31, September–October. https://isreview.org/issues/31/sds/

---

63. Armstrong 2001, p.107.
64. The International Socialists were the precursor organisation of Socialist Alternative.

Belden Fields, A 1988, *Trotskyism and Maoism: Theory and Practice in France and the United States*, Autonomedia.

Cleaver, Eldridge 1969, "On the Ideology of the Black Panther Party", *Black Panther Newsletter*, https://abolitionnotes.org/eldridge-cleaver/bpp-ideology

Cliff, Tony and Ian Birchall 1968, *France – the struggle goes on*, first published as a pamphlet in August 1968. https://www.marxists.org/archive/cliff/works/1968/france/

Dann, Jim and Hari Dillon 1977, *The Five Retreats: A History of the Failure of the Progressive Labor Party*. https://www.marxists.org/history/erol/1960-1970/5retreats/

Elbaum, Max 2002, *Revolution in the Air: Sixties Radicals Turn to Lenin, Che, Mao*, Verso Books.

Elbaum, Max 2024, "The Energy Has Changed. The Underlying Politics Have Not", *Convergence*, 31 July. https://convergencemag.com/articles/the-energy-has-changed-the-underlying-politics-have-not/

La Gauche Prolétarienne 1969a, "The J.C.R. in May–June 1968", *Cahiers de la Gauche Prolétarienne*, 1, April. https://www.marxists.org/history/france/post-1968/gauche-Prolétarienne/cahiers-04-1969.htm

La Gauche Prolétarienne, 1969b, "Blow for Blow", supplement to *La Cause du Peuple*, no. 20. Translation accessed from https://www.marxists.org/history/france/post-1968/gauche-Prolétarienne/couppourcoup.htm

Gitlin, Todd 1987, *The Sixties: Years of Hope, Days of Rage*, Bantam Books.

Herouvim, John 1984, "Politics of the Revolving Door: the Communist Party of Australia (Marxist-Leninist)", *Melbourne Journal of Politics*, 15, January.

Hill, EF 1959, *Builders of Communism: a report on the 21st Congress of the Communist Party of the Soviet Union*, Current Book Distributors.

Kelley, Robin DG and Betsy Esch 1999, "Black Like Mao: Red China and Black Revolution", *Souls*, 1 (4), pp.6–41.

Khrushchev, Nikita 1956, "Speech to 20th Congress of the C.P.S.U", delivered 24–25 February. https://www.marxists.org/archive/khrushchev/1956/02/24.htm

Lévy, Benny 1971, "Investigation into the Maoists in France", interview translated by Mitchell Abidor. https://www.marxists.org/archive/levy-benny/1971/investigation.htm

Lin Biao 1965, *Long Live the Victory of People's War*, Foreign Languages Press, 3 September. https://www.marxists.org/reference/archive/lin-biao/1965/09/peoples_war/index.htm

Linhart, Robert 1978, *The Assembly Line*, translated by Margaret Crosland, University of Massachusetts Press.

Lovell, Julia 2019, *Maoism: A Global History*, Bodley Head.

Mao Zedong 1964, *On Khrushchev's Phoney Communism and Its Historical Lessons for the World: Comment on the Open Letter of the Central Committee of the CPSU*, Foreign Languages Press, 14 July. https://www.marxists.org/reference/archive/mao/works/1964/phnycom.htm

Mao Zedong 1966, *Quotations from Chairman Mao Zedong*, Peking Foreign Languages Press. https://www.marxists.org/reference/archive/mao/works/red-book/

Johansson, Perry 2012, *Saluting the Yellow Emperor*, Koninklijke Brill NV.

Marx, Karl and Friedrich Engels 1845, *The Holy Family*, chapter 4, translated by Richard Dixon (1956), Foreign Languages Publishing House, Moscow. https://www.marxists.org/archive/marx/works/1845/holy-family/ch04.htm

Morris Jr, WB 1970, "Some Aspects of the Origins of the New Left", *Proceedings of the Oklahoma Academy of Science*, 50, 5 February, pp.187–90.

O'Lincoln, Tom 1985, *Into the Mainstream: The decline of Australian Communism*, Stained Wattle Press.

Peking Review 1953, "Statement by the Spokesman of the Chinese Government: A Comment on the Soviet Government's Statement of August 21", 6 (36), 1 September, p.9.

Programme and Constitution of the Revolutionary Communist Party USA, 1975. https://www.marxists.org/history/erol/ncm-3/rcp-program/index.htm

Progressive Labor 1969, "Panthers Unite with CP Hacks", 7 (3), November. https://marxists.architexturez.net/history/erol/1960-1970/plponpanthers.htm

Reid, Donald 2004, "Etablissement: Working in the factory to make revolution in France", *Radical History Review*, 88, 1 January, pp.83–111.

Rekret, Paul, Eoin O'Cearneigh and Patrick King 2022, "Introduction to Robert Linhart: Concrete Analyses in the Spider's Web of Production", *Viewpoint Magazine*, 5 December. https://viewpointmag.com/2022/12/05/introduction-to-robert-linhart-concrete-analyses-in-the-spiders-web-of-production/

Russell, Lani 1999, "Today the students, tomorrow the workers! Radical student politics and the Australian labour movement 1960–1972", PhD thesis, University of Technology, Sydney. https://www.marxists.org/history/erol/australia/students.pdf

Scheer, Mort 1975, "The History of the Progressive Labor Party – Part One", *Progressive Labor*, 10 (1), August-September. https://www.marxists.org/history/erol/1960-1970/plhistorynotes.htm

Smith, Evan 2022, "Ted Hill, The Khmer Rouge and Australian Maoism 1977–1980", published at the *New Historical Express*, 17 January. https://hatfulofhistory.wordpress.com/2022/01/17/ted-hill-the-khmer-rouge-and-australian-maoism-1977-1980

Smith, Jason E 2013, "From Etablissement to Lip: On the Turns Taken by French Maoism", *Viewpoint Magazine*, 3, 25 September. https://viewpointmag.com/2013/09/25/from-etablissement-to-lip-on-the-turns-taken-by-french-maoism/

Trotsky, Leon 1937, "Stalinism and Bolshevism", *Socialist Appeal*, 1 (7), p.5. https://www.marxists.org/archive/trotsky/1937/08/stalinism.htm

UJCml (Union des jeunesses communistes marxistes-léninistes) 1968, "On établissement". Translated by Jason E Smith, *Viewpoint Magazine*, 3, 25 September 2013. https://viewpointmag.com/2013/09/25/on-etablissement-1968/

Weinberg, Jack and Jack Gerson 1969, "SDS and the Movement: Where Do We Go From Here?", *Independent Socialist*, 12, September. https://www.marxists.org/history/erol/ncm-1/is-sds-split.pdf

MATT LAIDLAW

Why the Kenyan youth revolted: interview with a Kenyan socialist

Matt Laidlaw is a socialist based in Melbourne.

K ENYA HIT GLOBAL headlines earlier in 2024 when an unprecedented youth rebellion shook the government of William Ruto. Unprecedented is a worthy description for this event in a country once renowned as one of the most stable in the world – let alone in the region of East Africa. This stability was promising enough that Kenya became a major non-NATO ally of the United States this year (ironically, mere days before this rebellion began).

Kenya is an oligarch's dream when it comes to inequality. Oxfam reports that the wealthiest 0.1 percent of the population have more wealth than the bottom 99.9 percent combined. Official estimates of Kenya's youth unemployment sits around 13 percent for those *actively* seeking work; including the long-term unemployed, the number rises significantly, in a country where 59 percent of the population are below the age of 24.[1] This volatile and grinding reality makes it little wonder that youth revolted in their hundreds of thousands. Yet this rebellion took both the Kenyan rulers and the commentariat by surprise.

Kenya may be remembered among progressive people as a country with a radical anti-colonial history, owing a lot to the Mau Mau Revolt of the 1950s. Since then, it has been a sinkhole for radical politics. The

---

1. National Council for Population and Development 2024.

early radical leaders were either absorbed into the ruling elite, or assassinated. It was not until the 1990s that a mass campaign broke through, demanding multi-party elections and the opening of democratic spaces. The movement won, and the "stability" of Kenya's politics returned. *How* and *why* have Kenya's rulers managed to keep such a rotten state of affairs without trouble from below?

To explain this, Ezra, central committee member of the Revolutionary Socialist League in Kenya, sat down with *Marxist Left Review* to discuss the recent period of politics in Kenya. Ezra describes how the contours of politics today were shaped decades ago, and how the youth rebellion has ultimately disrupted that status quo.

∗

> **Matt:** *In 1992 Kenya moved away from the system of one-party rule that had seen the Kenya African National Union (KANU) ruthlessly control the country for decades. Why did this transition to multi-party elections occur, and what were the limits of democratisation?*

Ezra: Kenya got independence in the 1960s, 1963 to be exact. The first president after independence was [Jomo] Kenyatta. He ruled the country as a puppet of the British and it was just a neocolonial government. In 1978 [Daniel Arap] Moi took over and he followed in the footsteps of President Kenyatta. Moi unleashed a wave of repression in 1982 after there was an unsuccessful military coup against him by some sections of the Kenyan Air Force.

It is in this context that the single-party state was introduced, along with rampant repression. Around this time neoliberal policies were also being enforced in the country.

So Kenya was a one-party totalitarian state in the 1980s until the formation of the Forum for the Restoration of Democracy (FORD) Kenya and the emergence of underground youth leaders, student voices and some left forces that came together to fight for the multi-party state in Kenya. We call this struggle for democracy the second liberation of the country.

In terms of the leaders of the movement, most of them are now leading politicians in Kenya. There have been attempts by some people to whitewash the history of the democracy movement and argue that the movement was mostly revolutionary. However only a very small percentage of those involved were actually socialist, or revolutionary. Most of them were just pro-democracy and several of them are government ministers or governors now. Raila Odinga for example, he is dubbed as the hero of the multi-party fight in Kenya, but look at him now, he is just an imperialist, together with [William] Ruto – Ruto was also an active politician in the '90s.

It was in 1992 that multi-party rights were won: Section 2A of the Kenyan constitution, a section added by Moi in 1981 to enshrine one party rule, was repealed. This allowed people to form legal opposition political parties. The ruling party since independence had been the Kenya African National Union (KANU) and Ruto was in KANU then. You can see, he's never been on the right side of history in Kenyan politics, he was a Moi sycophant.

Raila was in the opposition, as were several governors, like the governor in my home county of Kisumu. He was a leader of the multi-party democracy, as was the governor of Siaya. They've since sold out, I don't know, they got old or something. The major factors that drove the movement were the extreme repression of the Moi regime and the introduction of neoliberal measures, increasing economic misery for most people.

> **Matt:** *It certainly seems like those two factors combined – the relationship that Kenya had to the US, and some of the debt restructuring, put pressure on allowing limited democratic rights. The other side of it is the mass movement, called Saba A.[2] What were the politics of the groups that organised the Saba A movement?*

Ezra: We still celebrate Saba A Day, to commemorate the heroes and celebrate Kenya's second liberation. The Saba A movement was made

---

2. The name Saba Saba refers to the Swahili date the protests began in 1990. Saba means seven.

up of leaders like Kenneth Matiba, Charles Rubia, Raila Odinga, Willy Mutunga, Anyang Nyong'o and many others.[3] It was a conglomerate of professionals. With literacy levels in Kenya in the '90s being so low, professionals, students and mainly the elites were the ones who took charge of political movements.

I am in contact with some of the activists from this movement, they talk about the underground organisation called the December 12 Movement, the DTM. DTM said they were socialist and revolutionary, and they even had study cells just like we do today and like you in Australia. You know, they were planning for a revolution and stuff like that, but they were infiltrated by government agents, and some were killed. In the end a number of them sought out asylum in Europe and America because of this.

For Saba Matia, the politics of the main groups and the leadership were not socialist, at best you could describe them as reformists. We cannot say that Raila Odinga had been a revolutionary. We can say his father [Oginga Odinga] was a little bit more radical, not a Trotskyist like us, but he was a little bit more of a socialist because he stayed true to himself until the time of his death. He championed the fight for a socialist state. However, by the beginning of Saba Matia, he was far too old to participate and was under house arrest, which he remained under until his death. For the movement the overwhelming focus of the politics was on the democratic reforms, and the revolutionaries had very little influence.

> **Matt:** *Who have been the major political players in Kenya since then?*

Ezra: The main political forces in Kenya since 1990 have gone through some degree of metamorphosis but largely the players are just the same. For example, Moi used to say KANU would rule for 100 years, and many

---

3. This short list gives an insight into the profile of the political leaders of Saba Saba. At the time Matiba was a politician, as was Rubia. The other three were all lecturers at University of Nairobi, Odinga just having spent some years in prison. Only Willy Mutunga had radical politics, being a part of the December 12 Movement, an avowedly Marxist intellectual group.

would argue today he is right, as so many of the KANU politicians of the Moi-era are still the people ruling Kenya today.

So, KANU was the main political party because it was the only legal party in the 1980s and the '90s. So, in 1992, when multi-party was introduced, there was an election where KANU, though very unpopular, still won because the opposition was divided. They split the forces, which allowed KANU to win, and Moi to continue ruling.

In the '90s KANU was still there. Although it was dwindling, it was still the main party alongside the National Development Party (NDP). The NDP was formed by Ralia Odinga in 1997. Ralia's father had been the leader of Forum for the Restoration of Democracy–Kenya (FORD–Kenya), which is still one of the major political parties in Kenya. After his death, Kijana Wamalwa took over the leadership of the party and so Ralia left to form the NDP which was a liberal-democratic party. In the 1997 election Moi won by dividing the opposition again and the NDP came third.

Coming forward to 2002, the people are getting more and more sick of the Moi regime, he had ruled for 20 odd years at this point. It was in 2002 when everyone had had it. The 2002 elections were defined by everyone against Moi, and everyone turned up. I think I was around 8 years old; I can remember some of it. In 2002, Moi lost by a large margin. That was not just the end of 24 years of Moi's rule, but the first time KANU was not running the country since independence.

Before being kicked out of power Moi had endorsed [Uhuru] Kenyatta [the son of the first President of Kenya] as his replacement. Kenyatta was still young at the time, so I think Moi just wanted him to get some exposure. Mwai Kibaki won in 2002 with the support of Raila Odinga, Charles Rubia and others who were at the forefront of the multi-party elections campaign.

Coming out of this, they formed the National Rainbow Coalition Kenya, NARC. NARC was led by Kibaki. Kijana Wamalma was made vice-president. Raila was in government under Kibaki, he was appointed the Minister of Roads.

Fast forward to 2005, we had a referendum because there was talk of a new constitution.[4] The fight over the changes to the constitution gave birth to the Orange Democratic Movement (ODM).[5] Raila had fallen out with Kibaki in 2005, and he formed ODM. Raila led the campaign against the new constitutional changes and then he used the party in the election in 2007 against Kibaki's own newly formed party, called the Party of National Union. Kibaki had ditched his own party as well that he previously ran with in 1997, called the Democratic Party. So, in 2007, Kibaki was very unpopular, but he rigged the elections because there is no way he won. Raila Odinga won the elections, everyone voted for him, but Kibaki had impunity, so Raila lost.

Following the fraudulent elections, in 2008 there was the outbreak of ethnic violence when thousands of Kenyans were killed. Raila Odinga was brought in to form a government of national unity with Kibaki. This is a common strategy of Raila across his career. He had done this with Moi in 2000 – when he was given a cabinet spot, and even elected secretary-general of KANU. He was hoping to be named as Moi's successor, but Moi decided to pick Uhuru Kenyatta. That is when Raila decided to jump ship and ally with Kibaki.

The next milestone was in 2010, when the new constitution was brought in, which was largely about devolving power to county governments. Then in 2013, Uhuru won, and then again in 2017. Both times Uhuru was running against Raila. The 2022 election was when Ruto came to power.

So, technically, the KANU boys have been president except the years Kibaki ruled. Of course, it should be remembered that Kibaki was also in KANU earlier on, and was the vice-president under Moi's regime at one point. Basically, everyone who has been president of Kenya has been in KANU at some point in their political career, even if they have gone on to form other parties.

---

4. The proposed constitutional changes of 2005 were narrowly rejected for fears of increasing presidential power as well as the growing unpopularity of the Kibaki regime.
5. The "Orange" in Orange Democratic Movement inspired by the symbol used in the referendum ballots to symbolise a "No" vote on the proposed changes. "Yes" votes were symbolised by a banana.

> **Matt:** What you are saying is all the political players after 1992 were the same as before the democratisation. The introduction of multi-party elections is described as this monumental change – like you were saying for a lot of people, this is like a second independence – but at the same time, everything at the top of society sounds like it just runs the same. Why do you think that that was the case?

Ezra: Well, you know in the forest, the apples don't fall very far from the tree. You see these forces of change, or that is how they want to seem, always have the same interests. These are people who have known each other since school. For example, Kalonzo Musyoka, who was vice-president under Kibaki, and is now the leader of one of the major parties in Kenya, was a minister under Moi in the 1980s. [William] Ruto for example was in KANU for many years, joining in 1990 under Moi, until 2007, and even after leaving KANU would serve in Uhuru Kenyatta's governments later. They are all the same players, you know, they just keep shifting goalposts, but they're the same guys, because their interests are the same.

When it comes to political ideologies, they're just right-wing neoliberals. Some may come out of progressive forces, but when they get any sniff of power it is just the same story every time. That's why we are getting into this cycle. They use their relationship with imperialist powers, who tend to have influence in Kenyan politics. I think the imperialist interests usually approve of these politicians, because they know they will further their agenda in this country, so that's why they usually are the same people since the 1980s.

> **Matt:** Why do you think it is the case that only people in or around KANU became the beneficiaries of the movement, and the more open political field?

Ezra: In my opinion, I think the literacy rates were very low, the majority of Kenyans did not get a chance to go to school in the 1990s. It was not until Kibaki came to power that primary education was made free. Basic ignorance was so widespread that it was very easy for the ruling class to fool the people. I think that's why, you know, they could recycle the same players. The issue of illiteracy is still there, but it was on a larger scale a few decades ago.[6] Things have shifted on that front now we have the internet, it is the information age, it is hard for politicians to lie to the people like that.

> **Matt:** *I suppose the other part of the question is that you had this big movement, with protests, strikes and riots in the 1990s, but it seems like the left didn't become a political force out of this. Did the left play a role in the movement, and have they played one since?*

Ezra: Even during the fight for multi-party democracy, there was no real left. The most radical left-wing organisation that I knew of was DTM. They were very small, with a membership of less than 100, and they were underground. You know, they couldn't even do their activities because Moi's regime was far more repressive than even Ruto's. People were getting killed. DTM died down as most of them went into exile in other countries.

There are other figures who are portrayed as on the left, like James Orengo, Raila Odingas and Co.[7] All of them turned out to be right-wing. None of them were really as left as they portrayed themselves to be in the early stages. Unfortunately, Raila is still often portrayed as a social-democrat, the left-wing, pro-welfare choice in politics – none of which is true.

The most radical people did not have the same platforms that the right-wing politicians had. Moi had been very repressive to leftists

---

6. Kenya's adult literacy rate sat around 74 percent in 1990, which has since risen to 83 percent in 2022. The secondary school enrolment rate however sat at 29 percent in 1990, doubling to 59 percent by 2009. The last year data is available on this. In university enrolment, the divide is even starker. Only 1 percent of the population were university-educated in 1990, with a student population of about 40,000. Today it is closer to 12 percent, with over 500,000 enrolled students domestically. See Kimalu et al 2001, Kenya National Bureau of Statistics 2023 and UNESCO Institute for Statistics 2024.
7. James Orengo (b. 1951) was yet another one of Saba Matia leaders from the University of Nairobi, following a similar pattern of student activist to university lecturer. He is now Governor of Siaya County.

during his rule. Raila Odinga's father, Oginga Dinga was imprisoned. Mind you he was not as left as you or me, more like a bureaucratic Stalinist, but was still seen as a threat. However, they did not have the same resources as the right-wing sections of the movement and faced serious repression.

> **Matt:** One of the other aspects of Kenyan politics that gets talked about a lot, especially internationally, is the role of ethnic or tribal based politics. There have been serious race riots following elections in the past for example. How do those politics operate and what is the importance of them in Kenyan politics?

Ezra: Tribal politics, tribalism, has been the key factor in organising among the ruling class since independence. For elections, people are galvanised, and organised according to their tribes. I was reading a paper recently about the national question in Kenya, and the truth is that the ruling class uses tribe as a barrier for people, in order to make it difficult for people to realise that the class struggle is the primary struggle that the people have.

So, tribalism has been very, very important in Kenya. Ruto is not the president because he is the best candidate, he is the president because he literally comes from one of the biggest tribes in the country, and he teamed up with the other biggest tribes in the country.[8] People vote in blocks, by their tribe, rather than according to their political ideologies like what I saw in Australia.

That is going to change, because the young generation is more aware, and you can see what happened in June, the protests were carried out by all youth of all tribes. The trajectory of politics is shifting away from tribalism. For now it is still important, but slowly by slowly it is going to die down. I know in the next election in 2027 tribe will still

---

8. The 2022 election saw Ruto narrowly win with 50.5 percent, to Raila Odinga's 48.9 percent. Ruto secured a strong vote among the ethnic Kikuyu, who have predominantly been strong backers of Kikuyu ex-President Uhuru Kenyatta. Uhuru, alongside powerful figures in the Kikuyu community, had endorsed Raila – foreshadowing the breakdown in strength of ethnic-tribal based political allegiances. See Nantulya 2022.

be a very big factor, but I think there will be voices of reason also, slowly by slowly it will be challenged.

> **Matt:** For those who are unfamiliar with how tribal politics operates, could you explain the impact that has for activists and socialists trying to organise resistance?

Ezra: Look, it has had a demobilising impact, it is very sad, but we tend to not try and blame the individuals, as this tribal lens of politics is very much conditioned into people. For organisers like us it is hard for us to penetrate, and it was hard to get through people who had predetermined minds.

You know, some politicians could even kick babies in the streets and still get votes, they could steal billions of [Kenyan] shillings, and they still get votes. It is not really supporting politicians based on what they represent for the people. It is more like fanaticism, like how you support your football team, that's how people support their politicians. With that kind of die-hard following, you can imagine how hard it is for people trying to organise a majority of the people when that is how they think.

> **Matt:** For the ruling class, you were saying tribalism is a way that they can help pacify people, a divide and rule strategy. Are there also uses for tribalism within the ruling class? I have read articles that suggest that it is a way of creating patronage networks, offering jobs, and regenerating cliques of the elite.

Ezra: So, if your people are in government, you get more development funding, you get infrastructural development in your area. Your people are the first in line to get jobs. The deputy president once said the government is a shareholding entity, where the people who vote and support are the first to benefit.

So, people in areas that are perceived to be in opposition have low development rates. You can see it in the type of roads there. If one day you ever come to Kenya, you'll see when we take a road trip, you will just realise just by looking around that this place is predominantly an opposition zone, because that's where the good road ends.

The change in the constitution in 2010, which devolved much of the power of the federal government to the county level with there being now 47 counties. Along with this much of the corruption has also been devolved, it did not stop corruption.

> **Matt:** *Another important factor in the past has been the role of student struggles. Students were important in the battles of the 1990s. Can you give us a picture of student struggles from the 1990s to today?*

Ezra: Yeah, right now the student struggle has really died down. There is a campaign that we are a part of organising currently in response to the killing of student union democracy. Ruto's government introduced a delegate system for student union leadership, which means students literally have no say in who their leaders are, which has pacified them.

It is hard to organise a demonstration today, like we used to in the '90s. Most of the leaders that we mentioned in the multi-party democracy fight in the '90s were student leaders. James Orengo was from the university, most of them came from the university, even Raila Odinga was a lecturer at the University of Nairobi then. So, this thing mainly sprouted from the university. It was very radical at the university campuses. Famously even one revolutionary student leader was killed on campus, there were demonstrations and solidarity on the campuses. That is a response we do not see now.[9]

In Australia for example, you organise protests for Palestine, but that kind of activism has been taken out of the student movement in Kenya. Yet during the struggle for a multi-party system, the main source of resistance came from the student movement – which shows the importance of this struggle that we fight to rebuild today.

---

9. In December 1996, student activist Festus Okong'o Etaba was murdered by police while protesting the overcharging of university fees.

> **Matt:** *When we spoke last, you were saying that this was not the first time the government has attacked student unions, or student voting rights. Has this been an ongoing battle in the student movement?*

Ezra: They have been trying for many years, they tried to pass the same restrictions around 2016, but people revolted, and the attacks receded. So, they chose to pass the attacks when everyone was on holiday, it was rushed through, so students could not come to school and demonstrate. It was hard before, but the fight is even harder now because there is no direct connection with student leaders and leaders are there now.

> **Matt:** *Since the struggles of the '90s, are there issues that you find motivate young people to get politically active?*

Ezra: The '90s were a little bit different because the problems and the reasons for picketing did not limit themselves to only school matters, you know, like fees and repealing the delegate system. They transcended the problems of the nation to bad governance, to fighting for the multi-party system, all led by students. On the contrary right now, if there is any resistance, the focus stays within the school premises and student problems.

What we want to bring back is the ability for students to be the voice of change, you know, they still have their youth on their side and they're very vocal, so they can be at the forefront in leading these demonstrations for all types of struggles.

> **Matt:** *Student activism is more campus-based and less outwardly political?*

Ezra: Yes, yes, it's just campus based. We have a lot of geopolitical issues happening, the war in Ukraine, the conflict in Palestine and you don't find any students participating in that here. That shows the level of political awareness and political consciousness among the students. It is very low compared to the past, the government has succeeded in pacifying them.

> **Matt:** Looking at Kenya's ruling class today, Ruto has been trying to assert Kenya as an important player in international politics, particularly for the Western bloc. What kind of role do you see Ruto pushing for Kenya to play?

Ezra: Yeah, I think especially during Ruto's time he has been positioning himself as the pointman of Western imperialism in sub-Saharan Africa, especially in East Africa. In the South of the continent you have South Africa, in West Africa we have Nigeria and Ghana, so he wants to position himself as, you know, the pointman for Western imperialism in the East, so he cosies up to Germany and other Western leaders. Recently Ruto visited Germany, where he talked about Kenyans being given 250,000 jobs in Germany, which was a complete lie. That's what he does, just lies.

Most people in Kenya are not fond of Western imperialism. You know it was the IMF and their program that brought people to the streets this year. The government is just ignoring the people's plea and looking to the West. I'd say most people want to remain neutral or maybe even favour China and Russia. As revolutionaries we know these are not the solutions. But Ruto's big aim is to make Kenya an imperialist powerhouse in sub-Saharan Africa.

> **Matt:** Is that what is motivating their desire to lead the UN Peacekeeping Mission in Haiti?

Ezra: Yes. We also have "peacekeeping" forces in the Congo. Kenya troops are being sent into Haiti despite the resistance from the people, you know. I think there is money involved, so that's why they do that.

> **Matt:** If Kenya looks to Israel as an example, it shows that can prove your importance to Western empires, you get a lot of support for whatever you want to do. Kenya is clearly a strong Western ally, and that is historically consistent. China recently has upset the dominance of the US across the continent; has that been the case at all in Kenya?

Ezra: Ruto's regime has cosied up to the West more than the previous regimes of Kenyatta and Kibeki, who were more pro-China. Ruto was in China recently to secure some loans for some projects so he's trying to play both sides a bit, but majority of the time he's cosying up to the Western side. The Chinese influence in Kenya politics has been reduced since Ruto came to power.

> **Matt:** *Kenya this year has not just been in the international news for being aggressively pro-Western, but also because of a major youth rebellion. Kenya was long hailed as a very stable government in a region of the world that is known for waves of coups, rebellions and civil wars. Could you describe the impact on politics the past year of protests and resistance has had?*

Ezra: The rebellion this year turned a new leaf in Kenyan politics. I think this is the biggest rebellion in the country since the 1990s, and potentially since independence. The recent wave of rebellion has had a huge impact on politics, there is a paradigm shift in the way people see politics, rejecting tribalism and some objectivity is coming into it, especially in the young generation, who are the majority of the population. I can say that the biggest impact is the death of tribal politics. Specifically, it is the beginning of the death of tribal politics, which means that progressive organisations can organise within a better political environment.

As well, people are unlearning the misleading official histories. For example, unlearning that the Kenyattas were the heroes of independence, and learning instead that they were traitors of independence. People are learning about other African countries, the struggles of the people there, which fuel rebellions like this, and link those struggles of other countries to their own. We have a more informed and engaged mass arising in Kenya because of this wave of struggle.

For revolutionaries this was so exciting to witness and participate in, to see the spirit of resistance in all Kenyans. Even though the protests did not really win, this is just the beginning. A new era in politics is shaping before our eyes.

> **Matt:** Why do you think then it was "Gen Z", or this round of protesters, who were able to push past some of the limits of tribal politics and unite in a rebellion?

Ezra: This youngest generation are far more educated than any generation before them, and information is far more accessible than before. This makes it harder for leaders like Ruto, whose government propaganda is just total lies. People are more capable of critical thinking about it, and fact-check his lies.

In the '90s politicians would lie but there was only one TV station, and 80–90 percent of the population were illiterate. The age of information has really pushed through the barrier of tribalism and all political parties. That is why the younger generation is more informed and they demand better government. When they came onto the streets earlier in the year people were arguing, we do not want to just be migrants, forced to get jobs overseas, we want to change our country so we can live in Kenya, which is very encouraging.

So it is about the information that they have but also most of them have been pushed to their limits. Many of them are unemployed, where people with degrees are finding five years after graduation, even ten years after graduation, they cannot find a job. That is what we are looking at here, that is what pushes people to the limit because they have nothing else to do, but they have all the time on their hands. You can imagine so many of them being educated and unemployed for so long and the kind of tension that builds up.

> **Matt:** That sounds like the same dynamic for struggles across the Middle East and North Africa over the past decade. Young people are given an education and skills they cannot use, and no opportunities for even a basic standard of living.
>
> Speaking of employment and work rights, we should discuss the role labour unions have played in Kenyan politics. It is not commonly discussed, but Kenya has a history of radical unions, both in fighting for independence, or the radical unions in the port-city of Mombasa in the 1970s and '80s, who played important roles in forming leftist organisations. Since

> the ushering in of multi-party democracy, what has the union movement in Kenya been doing?

Ezra: Trade unions right now are a shadow of what they were in the 1960s and '70s, post-independence. Right now, they are just passive organisations with rich union leaders and no tangible strategy for the movement. Unions were absent in the struggle this year against the Finance Bill, there was no union that came out to support the Gen Z protests.

Last week [11 September 2024] there was a strike at the Jomo Kenyatta airport in Nairobi, led by one of the unions. The strike was in opposition to Ruto's plan to sell the airport to an Indian company, Adani, so there were protests because this came with layoffs. The union had one meeting with the minister, just one meeting, and a few hours later after the start of the strike, the strike was called off. Maybe these union leaders were paid off or maybe they were just lied to about job security. When it comes to trade unions, they are a shadow of what it used to be, it is a terrible situation.

> **Matt:** Is this the case for the unions over the past 20 or 30 years?

Ezra: The leaders of the three unions are the friends of the politicians, and some of them are the kingmakers of politicians.

> **Matt:** What role do you think revolutionaries like yourselves in the Revolutionary Socialist League (RSL) have in Kenya right now?

Ezra: I think it is educating the masses now. I think that's the main thing that we need to do, shift their understanding of politics. Left politics and socialist politics are very unpopular here. I think our main role as RSL is to get the masses, try and recruit as much as we can and create a vanguard.

> **Matt:** Chatting to you when the protests were raging earlier in the year, you remarked on how many challenges come up trying to find, talk to, influence and recruit people in such a dynamic movement – with all its street battles, repression and various other groups. Looking back at the movement this year, what kind of role was the RSL able to play? Was the group able to grow out of this?

Ezra: In terms of the people who joined it is a mix of inspiration and despair. Some of them drop off as fast as we gain them. That is the reality of it, but I know we are generally getting stronger.

> **Matt:** What have you seen motivating people to join your group?

Ezra: Yeah, there is a huge percentage that is interested in politics and they're organising and seeing how we do things. For several of them who joined the group, it was like a wave, and with any slight inconvenience they dropped off. It is a mixture of both the inspiration, but also many losing hope quickly.

> **Matt:** Is there anything else about politics in Kenya since the 1990s that is important for readers to know who are less familiar?

Ezra: I would say much as it has been a slow growth, we can see there are small improvements in democratic spaces in the country, but still, it is very slow growth. For the left movement in Kenya it is a story of decline. If we talk about the Trotskyists, we are still just as weak as we were in the 1990s. Our task is very difficult, it is like we are reinventing the wheel. We know it is difficult, but it must be done.

> **Matt:** Regarding the weaknesses of the left in Kenya, you outlined how they struggled during the movement of the 1990s, but why has the left struggled from then until now?

Ezra: As much as there has been an increase in the democratic space, Kenya is less repressive as that it was in the '90s. I think the left has shrunk because of this notion of a better life on the other side. There has been no firm leadership of the left since then and the ones who masquerade as leftist leaders are just there for their own benefits and not for the people. The left's weakness is both a result of sabotage from within and conditions here are well placed for the other side, there are great conditions in Kenyan politics for right-wing people to thrive.

> **Matt:** Any other final things you wanted to add?

Ezra: Well, there is now a light at the end of the tunnel. With young people politically shifting as I described, we have hope things will get easier for our movement going forward.

References

Kenya National Bureau of Statistics 2023, "Economic Survey 2023", September. https://www.knbs.or.ke/wp-content/uploads/2023/09/2023-Economic-Survey.pdf, pp.320–55.

Kimalu, Paul K et al, May 2001, "Education Indicators in Kenya", *Kenya Institute for Public Policy Research and Analysis*. https://repository.kippra.or.ke/handle/123456789/2872

Nantulya, Paul 2022, "Seven Takeaways from Kenya's Consequential Election", *Africa Centre for Strategic Studies*, https://africacenter.org/spotlight/seven-takeaways-from-kenyas-consequential-election/

National Council for Population and Development 2024, "State of Kenya Population Report 2024". https://drive.google.com/file/d/1OrSWvtiqhLfHEUN8KzN7TmBOwFEzGHJC/view

UNESCO Institute for Statistics 2024, "School Enrollment, tertiary (% gross) – Kenya). https://data.worldbank.org/indicator/SE.TER.ENRR?locations=KE

APRIL HOLCOMBE

Review: China in global capitalism

April Holcombe is a long-term socialist and activist living in Sydney.

Eli Friedman, Kevin Lin, Rosa Liu and Ashley Smith, *China in Global Capitalism: Building International Solidarity against Imperial Rivalry*, Haymarket Books, 2024

Introduction

COMPETITION BETWEEN THE United States and China casts a shadow across the face of the entire globe. Over the past few years, rivalry between the two powers has broken out into open and sustained economic warfare. The US and its allies are blocking China's access to critical technologies, especially silicon chips, while China strains to climb the value chain and maintain its global manufacturing dominance.

Moments of heightened tension foreshadow the much greater dangers to come: Nancy Pelosi's inflammatory high-profile visit to Taiwan in 2022, China's aggressive military exercises around the island in response, the Chinese spy balloon scandal of early 2023. These were followed by calmer periods of patched-up relations, with commitments to greater trade and "cooperation". But the trajectory moves inexorably back towards confrontation.

US-China tensions represent the most dangerous dynamic

of twenty-first century capitalism: the drive to war between huge economic and military – indeed, nuclear – powers. It is therefore urgent that anti-capitalists correctly understand this rivalry, and stand on the right side against it.

China in Global Capitalism: Building International Solidarity against Imperial Rivalry is a useful new book that will help radicals do both these things. Alongside an informative analysis of contemporary Chinese capitalism, imperialism and US-China rivalry, authors Eli Friedman, Kevin Lin, Rosa Liu and Ashley Smith offer a strong defence of genuine, consistent anti-imperialism. Their argument is clear: socialists everywhere must implacably oppose both the American and Chinese ruling classes, and fight for solidarity between the working classes and oppressed people of all countries.

The authors criticise three wrong positions in the West with respect to the US-China rivalry. The most widespread, common among social-democrats and liberal progressives, is to side with the liberal-democratic West against authoritarian dictatorships in China, Russia and Iran. This works as hypocritical, sweet-sounding cover for the crimes of history's bloodiest power: US imperialism.

The second position is what the authors call "unidimensional anti-imperialism". This rightly opposes Western imperialism, but to the exclusion of all others. The crimes and imperialist interests of China or Russia are downplayed or ignored, as they are "not the main enemy". Some even view these regimes as an "anti-imperialist" check on the US empire. At best, this muddies our solidarity with people in Ukraine, Hong Kong, Xinjiang, etc. At worst, it completely discredits the left in the eyes of people struggling under and against these regimes.

A third tendency goes much further, heaping glowing praise on the Chinese Communist Party. For them, China is already socialist or well on its way. This position, of a small but potentially growing number of Western Stalinists and Maoists, overlaps with the extreme nationalist Chinese diaspora such as the Qiao Collective who champion imperialist expansion (or as they call it, "re-unification").

In each of these positions, the working class is entirely written out of the picture. The authors argue that "all three groups are united by their enthrallment to state power. If the state is seen as the only actor capable of exercising agency, we are left with the bleak choice of picking one side of the capitalist rivalry: Washington or Beijing" (p.5).

China in Global Capitalism serves as a general education on China so that genuine leftists can rebut these viewpoints. Part one argues conclusively that China is a completely capitalist society and a major imperialist power. Part two explores the internal dynamics of class-divided China, focusing on the struggles of workers, oppressed nationalities and women. Parts three and four deal, respectively, with the development and character of the US-China imperialist rivalry, and the possibilities for building international solidarity from below.

China is capitalist and imperialist

China is a thoroughly capitalist society. This fact is still disputed in small pockets of the left, from the respected Marxist economist Michael Roberts[1] to the US Stalinist organisation the Party for Socialism and Liberation.

The book's authors point to the endless features of capitalism at work in China. The wealth of China's economy presents itself, in the words of Marx, as an "immense accumulation of commodities". China has its own tech giants, housing bubbles and private health providers. Hundreds of millions of Chinese workers produce goods for global markets, domestic purchase and advances in machinery. Their labour is exploited by a ruling class of fabulously rich state bureaucrats and private capitalists. Internal migration is controlled through the draconian *hukou* registration system, to maintain a pliable and mobile workforce with no real rights and protections.

Those who claim China is non-capitalist point to the strong, interventionist role played by its state in the economy. State ownership, however, is perfectly compatible with capitalist production. Indeed, states are indispensable for ensuring the smooth functioning of private industry, its overall profitability, and meeting the strategic interests of the ruling class as a whole. Most countries have experienced levels of state intervention equivalent to or exceeding modern day China: for

---

1. Roberts 2022.

example, wartime United States, postwar Europe, or 1980s anti-communist Taiwan.

The question is not whether the state intervenes in the economy, but to what – and to whose – end. "If bureaucrats and capitalists control the state, use it to make profit, and competition is its underlying logic, it remains capitalist...today, bureaucratic capitalists in China control the state and use its ownership and control over SOEs [state-owned enterprises] to enhance the global competitiveness of its national economy and corporations" (p.20).

China's state-owned enterprises (SOEs) may not be strictly for-profit ventures, but they play an important role in powering many of China's private industries, and its global infrastructure projects in Africa, Latin America and Central Asia. Workers in SOEs are subject to the same capitalist despotism of speed-ups, wage cuts and layoffs, while the bureaucrats who run them are handsomely rewarded.

Political leaders in the Chinese state are capitalists in their own right, using political power to enrich themselves and private wealth to access political power. The wealthiest 153 members of China's central government bodies – the National People's Congress and the Political Consultative Congress – had an estimated combined wealth of US$650 billion in 2018.[2]

China's state apparatus also plays the same role of any other capitalist state, using naked force and repression to serve capital against labour. Police and government-controlled unions operate together to suppress strikes and arrest worker leaders. In the landmark 2014 strike at the Yue Yuen shoe factory, Chinese riot police came to the aid of the Taiwanese factory-owners against 40,000 workers.

China is not only a capitalist society, but an imperialist power. By tracing China's accelerating integration into global capitalism from the 1990s onwards, the authors explain the true conflict between the US and China. Rather than an ideological clash between socialism and capitalism, or democracy and authoritarianism, it is about China's meteoric economic rise. China's new, indispensable position in world trade and production threatens the US and its allies' dominance in East

---

2. Hurun Report, *Global Rich List 2018*.

Asia. "Rivalry with the US is fundamentally, if not exclusively, a struggle over control of natural resources, technologies, markets, intellectual property – in short, the essential ingredients for ensuring competitive advantage, profitability and power within global capitalism" (p.25).

For the first few decades of boom, the Chinese ruling class had a cautious foreign policy, focusing on attracting investment and making money. It was entirely dependent on foreign investment, its economy still paled in comparison to the West, and its military even more so.

However, by the time current president Xi Jinping came to power in 2012, China was a different beast. Foreign investment as a proportion of GDP had passed its peak, and China's huge demand for raw commodities kept much of the global economy afloat through the GFC. The focus shifted to building up domestic consumption and investment, and increasing geopolitical weight. Xi's vision to achieve the "Chinese dream" of Great Power status represented the new ambitions for growth and expansion of the Chinese ruling class. This has necessarily brought China into more open conflict with the US.

The plan to become a Great Power has been multifaceted. The One Belt, One Road initiative aims to export capital and deepen investment ties with the Global South. The strengthening of the top Communist Party leadership and anti-corruption drive are intended to centralise decision-making across the vast country.

But in order to turn economic power into true hegemony in Asia, the Chinese ruling class needs a first-rate military. A large naval fleet and expanded nuclear arsenal are core planks in China's plan to break out from America's containment strategy in the Asia Pacific.

Advanced weaponry requires a cutting-edge high-tech sector: constant developments in AI, quantum computing, and most fundamentally, a reliable domestic base for silicon chip production. The Communist Party has been driving up the exploitation of Chinese workers to achieve this as rapidly as possible. Turning manufacturing power into technological power into military power is textbook, modern-day imperialism.

The leadership under Xi is ambitious, but victory is by no means assured. The recent economic slowdown exposes the fragilities in China's imperialist ascendancy. The Belt and Road Initiative has bitten off far more than it can chew: projects and investment funds have slowed as Chinese companies face major delays, construction flaws, corruption and debt concerns, and poor planning. Project funding in Southeast Asia is currently falling short by US$50bn.[3] Other hurdles to taking on the US include "increased indebtedness; overcapacity; ineffectual investment; corruption; an ageing, shrinking and increasingly expensive workforce" (p.43).

The one fault with the analysis in these chapters is the ambiguous suggestion that China was non-capitalist during the Mao era (1949–78). The authors are divided on this question: some think Maoism was state capitalism, but others, as expressed in the book, argue that "China's road to capitalism" (p.11) came through the 1980s market reforms of Deng Xiaoping.

The transition from Mao to Deng, however, was from one form of capitalism to another. This explains the earlier regime's obsessive development of the nuclear bomb, with zero regard for the peasants and workers who were sweated and starved. Oppression of national groups also occurred under Mao, as the book points out later (pp.80, 83). These were characteristic of a bureaucratic capitalist class caught in global military competition – albeit starting from an extremely low productive base.

Against a certain left tendency inside and outside China to see Mao as an egalitarian alternative to today's billionaire-communists, it is important to set the record straight.

Struggles in China

The transformative rise of China at breakneck speed has produced enormous social contradictions. *China In Global Capitalism* explores the class, gender and national faultlines of a rising China.

Mainstream discussion of China has little or nothing to say about the potential of internal resistance. So this book, which describes class struggle in the countryside, cities and workplaces, is a refreshing antidote.

The rural struggle in contemporary China is often overlooked.

---

3. Strangio 2024.

People in the countryside rarely fight to maintain the ancient ways of agrarian life. Instead, their grievances concern the little or no compensation they receive when land is sold out from under them by profit-seeking local bureaucrats. Some resistance has reached surprising heights. The 2011 Wukan uprising, for example, involved years of campaigning, and villagers in demonstrations fighting riot cops. Eventually, government officials were chased out of Wukan. Locals won better compensation for the sale of their land and even, temporarily, the right to elect the village leadership.

Far more consequential, however, is the struggle of the working class. The book does not recount the 1989 Tiananmen Square uprising, which involved millions of state-sector workers, but there are other books with the space to do it justice.[4] After the ruthless crushing of Tiananmen Square, state-sector workers took part in desperate rearguard struggles in the 1990s and early 2000s against massive layoffs and privatisations, of which the book provides useful detail.

More important has been the growth of a gigantic new working class drawn from the countryside, which now exists as a permanent urban class of factory and service workers. The authors rightly emphasise the labour struggles of these "migrant workers". Through the 1990s and 2000s, hundreds of millions were driven into new manufacturing and assembly plants. Over a generation, basic working-class consciousness fermented and culminated in the 2010–15 strike wave, as rising expectations intersected with labour shortages fresh after the Global Financial Crisis.

From 2015, a government crackdown on civil society, an expanded system of court arbitration and the downsizing of labour-intensive manufacturing saw the strike rate decline considerably. But the growth of new sectors, the rise of youth unemployment and the economic slowdown are creating new pressures towards struggle.

The 2022 battle in Zhengzhou against Foxconn management, who had locked two hundred thousand workers inside the factory's "closed-loop" COVID-zero production system, is a thrilling example of the continued potential. "Workers staged perhaps the largest revolt in a

---

4. See Hore 1991.

decade, with thousands engaging in fierce physical battles with security guards, 'big white' pandemic control workers, and the police. In the aftermath, Foxconn promised to pay 10,000 yuan to workers to *leave* – a huge victory for the rioters" (p.60). The "White Paper Revolution", a moment of nationwide political resistance against harsh lockdown measures, broke out almost immediately after.

Sexual oppression

Chapter four deals with women's oppression and the growth of a new anti-sexist consciousness. This is an important component of the nascent repoliticisation among educated, disaffected youth.

China is a deeply sexist society. Women are expected to care for elderly parents, work in worse-paid jobs than male workers, and bear children they cannot afford to raise. Anger at these and widespread male chauvinism has produced a new feminist sensibility in China, aimed against everything from beauty standards to sexual violence, job discrimination and childbearing expectations.

The authors describe anti-sexist consciousness emerging from a clash of economic and social transformations. On one hand, the destruction of the urban welfare state from the 1980s, and the lack of social rights for migrant workers in cities, has made the cost of raising children prohibitive. At the same time, women are more educated and integrated into public life and work than ever before. They have opportunities and aspirations far beyond the family home.

So even without the abominable practices of the one-child policy, fertility rates would have plummeted. Attempts to increase births by relaxing the one-child policy in recent years have failed. The government faces, from its point of view, a "social reproductive crisis". In other words, it will soon have too few workers to exploit and the "burden" of too many old people.

The chapter focuses strongly on this demographic crisis. Undoubtedly, there is a "pro-natalist" mood in the government. As well as lifting the one-child policy, it legalised having children out of wedlock in 2023(!), implemented a mandatory "cooling-off" period before divorce, and applied minor restrictions on abortion access.

These symbolic but reactionary measures increase pressure on women to have children as part of their "natural" and "patriotic" duties.

However, demographics are not the full picture of women's oppression. As the book mentions, the government must square its demand for more children with the need for (low-paid) female labour force participation, among the highest in the world. Anti-sexist anger is also levelled against general male chauvinism in society, such as beauty standards, and sexual violence as exposed in a series of #MeToo cases.

Arguably, the entry of tens of millions of women into urban factories over decades, as well as into the educated professions, would have produced anti-sexist consciousness no matter the government's social reproduction crisis – as it did during the women's liberation movements of the 1960s and '70s, when fertility rates were falling but still high.

Granted, the government's pushes are clearly making matters worse. Young women are angry at the hypocrisy and unfairness of modern Chinese capitalism and the CCP dictatorship. The CCP leadership therefore treats feminism as a subversive, unpatriotic "Western" ideology. Five leaders of the NGO Youth Feminist Activism were arrested in a high-profile case in 2015. Challenging sexism requires a freedom to organise that the CCP simply will not allow. It will certainly not allow women to expose the abuse perpetrated by China's ruling elite men. Tennis player Peng Shuai suddenly disappeared from public life after she accused former vice-premier Zhang Gaoli of rape in 2021. As such, the authors rightly argue: "China's class inequality, gender oppression and denial of democratic rights are not separate issues; they are profoundly interrelated (p.74)".

For now, only individualistic forms of anti-sexism are articulated, focusing on career advancement or "birth strikes". It may be a while before the authors' hopes of working-class anti-sexist struggle eventuates, but it is right to point in the direction of this immense power: "The combination of the state pressure for women to take up more reproductive labour and the economy's dependence on their labour will stoke resistance among women workers" (p.73).

National oppression

Chapter six deals with China's "national" questions: Tibet, Xinjiang, Hong Kong and Taiwan. China wishes to destroy internal "subversives" (Uyghur Muslims and Hong Kong democrats), and totalise control of crucial geopolitical corridors – into Central Asia (Xinjiang), into South Asia (Tibet), and into the Pacific (Taiwan).

The Tibetans and the Uyghurs of Xinjiang have long been oppressed by the central government. It uses brute force against them and dilutes their claims of national self-determination by encouraging the colonial settlement of Han Chinese (the dominant ethnicity representing around 90 percent of China).

In Xinjiang, the CCP has established a vast system of detention, forced labour and cultural annihilation of the Muslim Uyghurs. Some self-described leftists still claim that news of Uyghur oppression is Western propaganda. Yet the CCP took its anti-Muslim "War on Terror" in Xinjiang straight from the playbook of Western propagandist George W Bush.

The self-determination struggles of Hong Kong and Taiwan are premised more on the defence of political democracy and civil society than on cultural or linguistic differences (although they exist). For historical and geopolitical reasons, this takes the form of a separate national identity in Taiwan; in Hong Kong, the same spirit generally manifests as a local identity. Hong Kong's fight to defend democracy ignited the largest social struggles against the CCP since Tiananmen Square. As a reactionary imperialist ruling class, the CCP dictatorship crushing democratic aspirations anywhere is a disaster for the oppressed everywhere.

In each case, Western powers have used the self-determination struggles cynically. The US and its allies pretend to be defenders of democracy or opponents of genocide. But Western politicians, who cry crocodile tears for the Uyghurs, ship the weapons for genocide in Palestine. Democratic rights in Hong Kong are sacrosanct – but not in the United States itself, where Black Lives Matter or Gaza encampment protesters are met with tear gas and rubber bullets. Taiwanese sovereignty matters, but not that of Iraq, Afghanistan, or practically anywhere else.

The CCP in turn, can cynically exploit the West's cynicism. Speaking against a UK statement at the UN about human rights violations of Muslims in Xinjiang, China's UN representative Zhang Jun deflected effortlessly: "It is the UK that has seen a rise in racism in recent years... It is the US that is known for committing genocide against Native Americans... This list can go on and on! Your hypocrisy, darkness, and evil are the biggest obstacles to the progress of the international human rights cause".[5]

Some on the Western left swallow this hook, line and sinker. Others are less gullible, but squeamish about offering solidarity to mass movements for self-determination at the sight of a small number waving US or UK flags, as in the case of the Hong Kong movement. Right-wing, pro-Western tendencies in movements against the CCP must be opposed, but they are guaranteed to get an upper hand if the left discredits itself with equivocation, abstention or worse. "The international left must not stand on the sidelines of these conflicts. Anti-communist politicians in the West...can only relate to these movements in an opportunistic and self-serving manner... The international left, on the other hand, maintains principles of radical democracy, autonomy and self-determination for oppressed nations as well as racial and ethnic minorities." (p.100).

US-China rivalry

Since the end of the Cold War, the world has moved from the "unipolar" moment of unchallengeable US supremacy to an "asymmetrical multipolar order" (p.106). Not only China, but Russia, expand their sphere of influence. To a much smaller extent, countries such as Israel, Iran, Brazil and Saudi Arabia also have room for manoeuvre.

Yet the rivalry between the US and China, the two largest economies, looms large over the world system and is pushing towards the consolidation of "blocs". All major events become inputs into the US-China struggle for dominance in the Asia Pacific. Far away in Ukraine, Russia's invasion and war has deepened its dependence on China, and on the other hand, reinvigorated NATO and Europe's dependence on the US.

---

5. *Global Times* 2023.

The North Atlantic "defence" pact now counts Japan, Australia and the Philippines as "global partners" and officially deems China a "strategic challenge".

What has been called the "New Cold War" differs drastically from the old. The unprecedented integration of world trade and production makes direct conflict unthinkably costly in the immediate term. This informs the strategy, initiated by Trump and expanded by Biden, to incentivise corporations to produce in the US and reduce economic dependency on China.

Elaborate, interventionist economic policies on both sides are a sign of the serious preparations being made for war in the long term. Military budgets increasing year on year is another.

Two more chapters in this section deal with how the climate crisis and pandemic are fed by, and feed into, the imperialist rivalry. Military build-up is locking in unprecedented fossil fuel expansion. Even as China's renewable energy sector expands quickly, it continues to open new coal-fired power stations and sharply increase its oil and gas imports from Russia.

China's climate criminality has become a convenient scapegoat for do-nothing Western emitters. But as the authors note, since China is the preeminent global manufacturer, capitalists the world over bear responsibility. "As foreign direct investment pours into China... global emissions get logged as Chinese emissions….the associated emissions are not 'Chinese' but, in fact, those of global capitalism and its integrated economies" (pp.131–32).

The pandemic has shown that capitalist governments learn nothing in or from a crisis. The need for international cooperation was junked for international competition such as vaccine races instead. China's COVID-zero policy collapsed under the burden of costs to manufacturing and in the face of popular discontent. When they finally opened up, the Chinese ruling class did so with all the murderous disregard of Boris Johnson or Donald Trump.

International solidarity

In the chapters on international solidarity, the authors discuss the Chinese diaspora in the US. The very large Chinese student population in American universities has experienced some pockets of politicisation. Enrolments in arts and the humanities have expanded, as has engagement in campus protests and activism. Chinese graduate workers even played a notable role in a very successful strike at the University of California in 2022. The stereotype of Chinese international students as apolitical or timid is being challenged – a process radicals have observed on Australian university campuses as well.

International solidarity in a grander sense, however, is a much more daunting task. Even where the anti-imperialist left is small, we must participate in and build movements against Western wars and interventions, against the billions spent on military build-up, and against racism which, as tensions increase, will be directed against Chinese people. Our first obligation is to point out the hypocrisy, lies and crimes against humanity of our Western ruling classes.

Yet an understanding of, and implacable hostility to, Chinese imperialism, is indispensable. When China commits its own crimes against smaller nations, the Western left should not minimise this, but stand with those nations' right to self-determination. Secondly, oppressed people rising up against the Chinese Communist Party are neither part of a CIA plot nor unwitting Western pawns, but our siblings in the struggle for a better world. Lastly, certain diaspora such as hardline CCP loyalists in the West are anti-working class right-wingers from an oppressor nation. They are not allies for the left against Western imperialism.

Naturally, no great strategy can be laid out in this short book for building stronger, more direct ties between US and Chinese workers; the left is in no position anywhere to produce them. In the meantime, the authors argue that "a crucial way to deepen ties on the left internationally is organising discussions, meetings, teach-ins, and conferences about the conflict between the US and China and the urgency of organising international solidarity against it" (p.174). Such educational opportunities are welcome.

However, if eventually we want to move beyond the idea of

international solidarity to the concrete reality, we must also commit to building cohered revolutionary socialist organisations in our countries. Only with much greater numbers of activists across various countries can movements that emerge in one place spread over to, amplify, or be backed up by, movements in another. Such activists must be trained in internationalist socialist politics and involve themselves in the day-to-day struggles of workers and the oppressed. This is very difficult in China, where all independent political organising is strictly banned. In the West, where political freedoms are greater, our responsibility to take advantage of it is also greater.

Conclusion

China In Global Capitalism makes an urgent and compelling case for socialism from below against two imperialist powers preparing for catastrophic confrontation. It is a useful guide to China's place in the many issues that confront anti-capitalists today – climate destruction, women's oppression, national liberation, working class struggle. Such guidance is crucial as genuine socialists continue to do battle against old and new apologetics for imperialism.

"We must proclaim loudly and repeatedly that the fate of marginalized and exploited people around the world are in fact linked… The poor and socially vulnerable populations of Zhengzhou and New Orleans face the rising flood waters of catastrophic climate change, while the rich continue their lavish lifestyles safely barricaded in high rises or bucolic second homes. So now more than ever before, it is time to build the political and organisational groundwork for solidarity against the imperialist scramble for dominance over a global capitalism that threatens the well-being of the entire world" (pp.175–76).

References

Global Times 2023, "US, West 'hypocritical' in smearing China on Xinjiang but neglecting Palestinians' suffering", 19 October. https://www.globaltimes.cn/page/202310/1300197.shtml

Hore, Charlie 1991, *The Road to Tiananmen Square*, Bookmarks, London. (A new edition with an expanded introduction is soon to be published by Red Flag Books, Australia.)

Hurun Report, *Global Rich List 2018*, February. https://www.hurun.net/en-US/Info/Detail?num=2B1B8F33F9C0

Roberts, Michael 2022, "China as a transitional economy to socialism?", *Journal of Global Faultlines*, 9 (2), pp.180–97.

Strangio, Sebastian 2024, "China Infrastructure Pledges Falling Short in Southeast Asia, Report Claims", *The Diplomat*, 28 March. https://thediplomat.com/2024/03/china-infrastructure-pledges-falling-short-in-southeast-asia-report-claims/

LUCA TAVAN

Review: Zombie Kautskyism

Luca Tavan is a member of Socialist Alternative and contributor to *Red Flag* and *Marxist Left Review*.

Douglas Greene, *The New Reformism and the Revival of Karl Kautsky – The Renegade's Revenge*, Routledge 2024.

When Georges Haupt, an outstanding historian of socialism in the period of the Second International, on a visit to a Canadian university, wondered why students always referred to "renegade Kautsky," he learned that they believed "renegade" was Kautsky's first name.

DOUGLAS GREENE'S BOOK opens with this anecdote (p.1), which encapsulates Karl Kautsky's spectacular fall from grace. Once the intellectual leader of the largest socialist party in Europe, Kautsky died in relative obscurity in 1937. The decline of his influence mirrored the degeneration of German Social Democracy, the party to which he dedicated his life, which went from the great hope of socialism to a name synonymous with betrayal of Marxist principles. On 4 August 1914, this avowedly Marxist party voted to support the German war effort and rapidly transformed into a party of law and order. As a defender of the SPD and opponent of the 1917 Russian Revolution, Kautsky spent the rest of the twentieth century remembered best as one of the reformist foils of revolutionary socialists like Luxemburg and Lenin, the latter of whom gave him the moniker "Renegade" in one of his famous polemics.

Now, much like the controversial Britpop band Oasis, Karl Kautsky is going back on tour. Historians and socialist writers, including Mike Macnair and Eric Blanc, have exhumed Kautsky's writings, championing his pre-war Marxism as a model for socialist strategy. Common to these contributions is an attempt to rehabilitate Kautsky and historiographically reverse the rift which defined his era – the painful schism between revolutionaries and reformists that took place during the First World War. This rift left the socialist movement divided between two rival "Internationals" fighting for the allegiance of workers, and conditions of veritable civil war between revolutionary workers and a Social Democratic government in Germany.

At stake in the contest over Kautsky's legacy today are a series of age-old questions which have split the socialist movement since the time Karl Kautsky reigned supreme. What lines of demarcation should socialists draw in the organisations they build? What approach should socialists take toward imperialist war? Can the capitalist state be used as a vehicle for socialist transformation?

The New Reformism and the Revival of Karl Kautsky by Douglas Greene is an important contribution to the debates sparked by Kautsky's revival. Greene's book chronicles Kautsky's life and contributions, details his debates with rivals on the revolutionary left, and critiques the arguments of neo-Kautskyists who have attempted to restore his image.

Karl Kautsky: revolutionary?

The first section of Greene's book is a highly condensed political biography of Kautsky, charting his trajectory from the left of the socialist movement to the right. Greene's examination of Kautsky's record can help dispel myth-making about his supposedly "radical" early period as the internationally recognised guardian of Marxist orthodoxy.

Kautsky came to prominence as Germany's foremost Marxist theoretician at a turning point in the history of the socialist movement. In 1890, the German Social Democratic Party (SPD) was emerging from a long period of illegality under the regime of Otto Von Bismarck. The party had not only survived state repression but had successfully utilised loopholes in the law allowing participation in elections, winning 20 percent of the vote that year. Kautsky, who had built his name as editor of the illegal newspaper *Sozialdemocrat*, was commissioned to write a new Marxist program for the party.

The Erfurt Program was rife with ambiguity – it condemned capitalism, but shied away from an explicit challenge to the German state, instead emphasising a strategy of contesting parliamentary elections and a "minimum program" of day-to-day reforms that could guide the party's practice. Greene argues that the effect of this ambiguity on Kautsky's part was "to reconcile the conflicting camps of reform and revolution" (p.14).

Greene points to left radical Franz Mehring as an early critic of this parliamentary orientation, an outlook he described as "like a knife that lacks both handle and blade" (p.14). Mehring warned that the state would simply abolish universal suffrage if socialists came close to a parliamentary majority, rendering preparation for revolution necessary. However, these criticisms were largely drowned in the euphoria of the party's stellar advance and the general feeling among members, reinforced by Kautsky's positivist theoretical framework, that the future was assured for socialism.

In time, the SPD boasted a million members and more than 90 daily newspapers. It permeated every aspect of working-class life with youth organisations, socialist schools, sports clubs and cooperatives, and trade unions, which organised millions.

However, the peaceful growth of the SPD during a period of stability also led to the construction of a huge party apparatus: parliamentarians and their staffers, journalists, managers of the cooperatives and more. Alongside this apparatus, the unions spawned thousands of trade union officials. For many of these relatively comfortable apparatchiks, maintaining the party became an end in itself – they wanted class peace and party unity above all. These layers found their first coherent intellectual expression in the "revisionist" theorist Eduard Bernstein, who argued that capitalism's tendencies toward polarisation and crisis were diminishing, and socialism would be the outcome of a process of gradual reform.

While Kautsky defended Marxist orthodoxy against this theoretical offensive, his response conceded many points to Bernstein – most significantly agreeing to defer the question of how to achieve state power: "We can leave the decision on the problem of the proletarian dictatorship to the future. Again, we do not need to tie our hands" (p.28).

In substance, Kautsky reaffirmed the Erfurt consensus while allowing the reformist practice of party and union leaders to continue unchecked. As Greene writes:

> Many inside the SPD apparatus and labor unions shared Bernstein's views, but they were not willing to say the quiet part so loud. As SPD secretary Ignaz Auer wrote to Bernstein in 1899: "My dear Ede, one does not formally make a decision to do the things you suggest, one doesn't say such things, one simply does them" (p.28).

Union leaders engaged in daily compromise and collaboration with employers could continue their practice without the need for theoretical justification.

Kautsky's theoretical formulas aimed to maintain the unity of the SPD as a "broad church" socialist party just as it was increasingly divided between left and right. A series of debates in the aftermath of the 1905 Russian Revolution about the relevance of mass strikes in socialist strategy culminated in a conscious split between Kautsky and the radical wing of the party.

This conflict came to a head in 1910, when the refusal of the Prussian state government to abolish its undemocratic "three-class" voting system produced working-class outrage and boiled over into a series of mass demonstrations that met with brutal police repression. Rank-and-file workers who demanded an unlimited general strike to win electoral reform were met with hostility from the party bureaucracy, who declared the proposal "mass insanity".

Kautsky stood in these debates as a spokesperson of the "centre". While supporting the idea of mass strikes in principle, he argued that such struggle was "premature", and vetoed articles by radicals urging action. Kautsky justified his approach as a strategy of "attrition"

– urging the SPD to patiently build socialist forces and demoralise the enemy without provoking a fight. In essence, he advocated a gradualist approach, which meant subordinating class struggle to the exigencies of electoral cycles: "Today our agitation must escalate not towards the mass strike, but towards the coming Reichstag elections" (quoted on p.52).

Radicals were routed in the suffrage debate, evidence that the balance of power in the party was shifting decisively in the favour of reformists. Rather than fight this backsliding, Kautsky offered increasingly implausible theoretical salves to justify the party's passive parliamentary practice and internal paralysis.

As storm clouds of war gathered in Europe, Kautsky continued his struggle to reconcile the warring camps. While radicals urged anti-militarist agitation against the threat of impending conflict, and the party's right openly embraced German nationalism and colonial policy, Kautsky sat stubbornly in the centre. He developed a new, highly implausible theory of "ultra-imperialism" which claimed that, in the long term, peace was in the self-interest of the capitalist class. When the SPD decisively betrayed its socialist principles at the outbreak of World War I and voted for war credits, it revealed a deep rot, the product of years of conservatisation and integration into German capitalism. Kautsky initially refused to criticise this orientation, arguing that the war was nothing but a blip that would soon come to an end, allowing the party to continue its peaceful pursuit of a parliamentary majority.

Confronted with the reality of revolution at the height of the war Kautsky shrank away from the struggle for socialism. Leon Trotsky described his trajectory scathingly:

> So long as the class struggle flowed between the peaceful shores of parliamentarism, Kautsky, like thousands of others, indulged himself in the luxury of revolutionary criticism and bold perspectives: in practice these did not bind him to anything. But when the war and the after-war period brought the problems of revolution onto the field, Kautsky took up his position definitively on the other side of the barricade (quoted on p.117).

Kautsky opposed the October Revolution in Russia, the first attempt by workers to take state power – decrying the struggle as "premature" and complaining about the disenfranchisement of Russian capitalists. Revolution then spread to Germany in 1918, when a sailors' revolt sparked a working-class uprising which overthrew the Kaiser. As the reformist SPD entered a coalition government with capitalist parties and violently hunted down revolutionaries, Kautsky stood again in the centre, blaming both sides as "extremists" who mirrored one another. He urged a reunification of the socialist movement and the limiting of the revolution to securing a capitalist democracy. He spent the rest of his life a bitter critic of the new Communist movement which emerged from this period.

Greene draws this balance sheet of Kautsky's legacy:

> Despite his radical rhetoric, Kautsky quickly adapted himself to the parliamentary and reformist direction of Social Democracy. The limitations of Kautsky's Marxism appeared whenever it was necessary to offer concrete answers to pressing questions such as the nature of the state and the appropriate tactics for socialist revolution (p.5).

Kautsky's back

So why does this history matter? There are some today who claim Kautsky's theory can provide a guide to building socialist organisations and for revolutionary strategy. They want to salvage the "positive" elements of Kautsky's project and extract it from the logic of his later betrayal. The third section of Greene's book engages with the arguments of these "neo-Kautskyists", the most important of whom are Mike Macnair and Eric Blanc.

Mike Macnair is a leading figure in the Communist Party of Great Britain, who argues that the revolutionary left needs to draw its strategy from the high point of Second International Marxism. He identifies Kautskyism as the "golden mean" between reformism and the radical left: "I argue that the 'strategy of patience' of the Kautskyan centre was and is preferable to either the strategy of cross-class 'left' coalition government favoured by the right, or the 'mass strike strategy' favoured by the left" (quoted on p.193).

The American socialist Eric Blanc is the author of Revolutionary Social Democracy: Working-Class Politics Across the Russian Empire (reviewed in MLR 23), an extensive defence of Second International Marxism. Blanc has revived Kautsky in an attempt to unearth a credible and unblemished parliamentary socialism. He argues that Kautsky's greatest insight was that: "the path to anticapitalist rupture in conditions of political democracy passed through the election of a workers' party to government". Blanc sees Kautsky as an alternative to the strategy of Leninists, who "for decades have hinged their strategy on the need for an insurrection to overthrow the entire parliamentary state".[1]

Both are critical of Kautsky's eventual lurch to the right but argue that pre-war "Kautskyism" provides a model. But was Kautsky at his best good enough?

Macnair upholds Kautsky's strategy of patience as a guide for those who want to build revolutionary organisations today, writing: "I do not want to revive Kautsky, but a part of Kautsky, namely the serious, long-term attention he paid to the idea that before you get to the point of being able to pose the question of power, you have to build up a movement in non-revolutionary times" (quoted on p.193).

Kautsky's "patience" really meant subordinating workers' struggle to the project of gradually building a solid party apparatus and playing the parliamentary numbers game. This was expressed clearly in the mass strike debate of 1910, when a chance to qualitatively advance struggle was squandered as Kautsky advised socialists to "keep their powder dry" and wait for the next election.

Most revolutionary socialists would agree with Macnair's invocation to build movements in non-revolutionary times. Kautsky's gradualist strategy of "attrition", however, is a conservative strategy which ignores the reality of how radical working-class consciousness and organisation is built.

As US socialist Charlie Post explains in his contribution to the Kautsky debate:

---

1. Blanc 2019.

> [W]orking-class struggle under capitalism takes the form of massive and discontinuous upsurges. It is during these periodic upheavals that working people can win gains and build democratic organizations that cement solidarity and overcome the divisions and fragmentation of the class. To succeed, such movements always involve rising levels of confrontation with the established political and economic order and tend to radicalize many of their participants.[2]

The capitalist class and their state can't be gradually worn down through "attrition", but can only be defeated through great revolutionary upsurges, processes Trotsky described as the "forcible entrance of the masses into the realm of rulership over their own destiny".

Any socialist serious about uprooting capitalist society knows that it's necessary to win a majority. But attempting to appeal to a majority in non-revolutionary periods, when capitalist ideas predominate, can only produce compromise and political accommodation. Revolutionaries can only win a majority through intervention into the episodic struggles that radicalise their participants and turn the world upside down, as Rosa Luxemburg wrote in 1918:

> As bred-in-the-bone disciples of parliamentary cretinism, these German social democrats have sought to apply to revolutions the homemade wisdom of the parliamentary nursery: in order to carry anything, you must first have a majority. The same, they say, applies to the revolution: first let's become a "majority". The true dialectic of revolutions, however, stands this wisdom on its head: not through a majority to revolutionary tactics, but through revolutionary tactics to a majority – that is the way the road runs. Only a party which knows how to lead, that is, to advance things, wins support in stormy times.[3]

But both Macnair and Blanc dismiss revolutionary tactics in favour of a "parliamentary socialism" purportedly more suited to liberal

---

2. Post 2019.
3. Rosa Luxemburg, *The Russian Revolution*, quoted in LeBlanc 2020.

democracies of the West. Eric Blanc defends "Kautskyan" strategy in these terms:

> Even at his most radical, Kautsky rejected the relevance of an insurrectionary strategy within capitalist democracies. His case was simple: the majority of workers in parliamentary countries would generally seek to use legal mass movements and the existing democratic channels to advance their interests. Technological advances, in any case, had made modern armies too strong to be overthrown through uprisings on the old nineteenth-century model of barricade street fighting. For these reasons, democratically elected governments had too much legitimacy among working people and too much armed strength for an insurrectionary approach to be realistic.[4]

Blanc claims that he has no illusions that the capitalists would respect a socialist majority at the ballot box, and that a "decisive battle" of political and institutional rupture should be expected and prepared for. But what would this "institutional rupture" look like? While it's undoubtedly true that a left-wing government can presage sharp class battles as the 1936 election of the Popular Front government in Spain or Chile's Allende government shows, this only poses the question of how the working class can resolve this conflict – a question Blanc leaves unanswered.

Any party in parliament first faces the prospect of passive and active resistance to the implementation of any socialist measures not just from the private capitalist class, but also from the permanent, unelected state bureaucracy. The fate of the Allende government in Chile, overthrown by a bosses' offensive capped off by a coup organised by the military hierarchy, is a reminder of the danger of capitalist repression of elected government.

While Allende's Socialist Party remained "imprisoned in the bourgeois order" as one revolutionary critic described, the real alternative was posed by organs of popular control established by workers

---

4. Blanc 2019.

in the factories and neighbourhoods, which confronted capitalist sabotage, distributed goods, began organising production and undertook to arm workers.

To effectively block resistance from the capitalists, the bureaucracy and the military, these organisations of working-class power would have had to become a substitute state. This would mean breaking fundamentally with the democratic socialist strategy, by taking power against both the repressive wings of the state and the parliamentary socialists in government.

It's only in the context of workers' revolution, when capitalism is severely destabilised, that overthrowing capitalist states becomes a real possibility. As the Belgian revolutionary Ernest Mandel put it:

> These defences permit no lasting assemblies or sieges of long duration. They can be dismantled, but only at precise moments, when a juxtaposition of circumstances momentarily weakens or even paralyses the enemy's ability to make use of them. But this moment never lasts very long. It is called a "revolutionary crisis".[5]

Fundamentally, the contest between two rival political powers on the same territory can only be resolved by force, by the destruction of one or the other. The better organised and more clear-sighted the revolutionary forces, the less physical violence will be necessary to achieve that victory. This is the lesson of situations of "dual power" from Russia in 1917, to Spain in 1936, to Chile in 1973. It has been learned through innumerable revolutionary struggles that have shown the necessity of clearly breaking with the capitalist state.

Blanc's schema for socialist change, which urges an orientation to winning a parliamentary majority armed only with the vague notion of the need for a "rupture" with capitalism, is not based on any real reflection on the history of workers' struggle.

Mike Macnair justifies a parliamentary approach with an even more wildly unrealistic perspective, championing a "democratic republic" as

---

5. Mandel 1978, pp.192–93.

the political form necessary to carry out a socialist transformation. In his book Revolutionary Strategy, he summarises the program thus:

> Until we have won a majority (identifiable by our votes in election results) the workers' party will remain in opposition and not in government... When we have a majority, we will form a government and implement the whole minimum programme [ie of democratic reforms, LT]; if necessary, the possession of a majority will give us legitimacy to coerce the capitalist/pro-capitalist and petty bourgeois minority. Implementing the whole minimum programme will prevent the state in the future serving as an instrument of the capitalist class and allow the struggle to progress on terrain more favourable to the working class.[6]

While Macnair appeals to the authority of Marx and Engels to justify this position, they argued something quite different. Reflecting in 1891 on the lessons of the Paris Commune, Engels made it clear he considered even the "'purest' democratic republic" an organ of capitalist rule: "In reality..., the state is nothing but a machine for the oppression of one class by another, and indeed in the democratic republic no less than in the monarchy".[7]

Since the social content of every state has been to uphold the class rule of a minority, Marx saw that a working-class revolution would of necessity involve smashing and superseding the bounds of the bourgeois state. This was the significance of the Paris Commune, as Marx outlined:

> This was, therefore, a revolution not against this or that, legitimate, constitutional, republican or imperialist form of State power. It was a revolution against the State itself, of this supernaturalist abortion of society, a resumption by the people for the people of its own social life.[8]

---

6. Macnair 2010, p.50.
7. Engels 1891.
8. Marx 1871.

Socialists who reject an insurrectionary strategy for socialism can point to the difficulty of overthrowing modern capitalist states. But they can find no historical precedent that vindicates their strategy of a parliamentary road to socialism, and they most definitely cannot claim the authority of Marx and Engels to support their argument.

Kautsky's theory at its most radical can't provide a guide for smashing the power of the bureaucratic capitalist state and creating the forms of democratic self-government that can allow workers to run society. None of his epigones, either, have posed convincing answers to these questions within the framework of his theory.

If Kautsky at his best isn't good enough, there is a broader problem with Blanc and Macnair's method. They want to extract Kautsky's strategic arguments at a certain point in his political development (generally somewhere just before 1910), separated completely from his political practice. This is a thoroughly idealist and non-Marxist approach. Kautsky's theoretical formulas, as Greene's book shows, were shaped by a desire to reconcile opposing tendencies in a broad socialist organisation shifting rightward. His political backsliding followed the degeneration of the organisation he dedicated his life to defending. This degeneration had deep material roots, most extensively chronicled in Carl Schorske's book The Development of the Great Schism, which explains the SPD's bureaucratisation and integration into German capitalism. Although Kautsky shied away from the worst excesses of the SPD, his life's work was a defence of this process. His rejection of the mass strike tactic was a conscious concession to the army of conservative trade union bureaucrats that politically dominated the party. His distortion of the Marxist theory of the state muddied the task for socialists in a period of war and revolution. His urging of socialist "unity" allowed reformists to gain ground unimpeded, and then became a call to mend the necessary division taking place between opponents and supporters of capitalism.

Kautsky's contemporary critics, revolutionary Marxists like Vladimir Lenin, Leon Trotsky and Rosa Luxemburg, understood this. They criticised Kautsky not only for his increasingly explicit conservatism but for the role that he played in papering over clear divisions in the socialist movement, a practice that only benefited the movement's most open defenders of capitalism. From the perspective gained by witnessing the catastrophic collapse of Social Democracy during the war, Kautsky's long-term political deficiencies became clearer. The middle section of Greene's book illuminates how Kautsky's radical rivals understood his politics.

Revolutionary anti-Kautskyism

Rosa Luxemburg, the most formidable figure of the German revolutionary left, broke clearly with Kautsky during the mass strike debate of 1910, as Greene writes:

> Luxemburg concluded that Kautsky's "strategy of attrition" amounted to a "Nothing-But-Parliamentarianism". For the SPD, mass action was viewed as a "hindrance" to their "parliamentary and union daily routine". To prevent a disruption of this orderly strategy, she believed the SPD would use its organizational power to "put the brakes on the mass action" (p.90).

While Lenin's hostility to Kautsky only developed after the great betrayal of 1914, he took seriously the task of locating the roots of this disaster. In The State and Revolution, published in 1917, Lenin identified the source of Kautsky's political degeneration in his evasion of the question of state power. He accuses Kautsky of being deliberately vague about the nature of workers' power as far back as his 1902 pamphlet The Social Revolution:

> Throughout the pamphlet the author speaks of the winning of state power – and no more; that is, he has chosen a formula which makes a concession to the opportunists, inasmuch as it admits the possibility of seizing power without destroying the state machine (quoted on p.108).

In his polemic The Proletarian Revolution and the Renegade Kautsky, Lenin attacked Kautsky's tendency to approach democracy abstracted from its class character: "It is natural for a liberal to speak of 'democracy' in general; but a Marxist will never forget to ask: 'for what class?'"

(quoted on p.109). This is a criticism that could equally be levelled at Kautsky's modern epigones.

In Socialism and War, Lenin attacked Kautsky mercilessly for his role as representative of the "centre", attempting to elide principled differences between reformists and revolutionaries and prevent necessary political clarification on the questions of war and revolution:

"[T]he Kautskyan 'Centre' is doing more harm to Marxism than avowed social-chauvinism. Whoever now obscures disagreements, whoever now, in the guise of Marxism, preaches to the workers what Kautskyism is preaching, is lulling the workers."[9] Lenin argued that "centrists" like Kautsky were the greatest danger to the politics of the workers' movement, because unlike the avowed reformists, they refused to put their positions clearly.

This small sampling of the critiques outlined in Greene's book gives a sense of the questions at stake in the schism in European socialism. Kautsky's Marxist critics took him to task by exposing the links between his theoretical evasions and his conservative political practice. A similar critique should be made of the socialists who are today reviving his legacy.

Mike Macnair upholds Kautsky to further his argument for a broad party encompassing different tendencies that are committed to "Marxist unity". Macnair shares Kautsky's belief that the working class should have only one party:

> The proletariat as a class has an extremely powerful interest in common action among people who have political disagreements – which is necessary to trade unions and all other sorts of workers' organisations. Hence, setting yourselves up in organisational competition with existing workers' organisations to recruit individuals is a sure-fire route to marginality unless you have a very clear political explanation of why you have to be separate.[10]

Macnair counterposes the success of Social Democracy in its ascendant period to the trials and tribulations of small groups today. While

---

9. Lenin 1915.
10. Macnair 2020.

the challenges facing scattered groupings of revolutionaries today are immense, attempting to elide the principled differences and distinctions on the left that have emerged through a century of bitter experience can't create a shortcut to mass influence. It is impossible for socialists today to recreate the experience of Social Democracy at the dawn of the workers' movement – and nor should we try. Under the banner of "unity" these parties became dominated by reformist elements which converted them into bulwarks of capitalist stability. It is precisely on the basis of these experiences that revolutionaries have a "clear political explanation" of why they have to strive for organisational independence from reformists.

Macnair argues today that the radical left should focus almost exclusively on regroupment, deriding organisations that focus on individual recruitment and a "practice in which party activity means mainly 'activism': ie, running round from one agitational initiative to the next".[11]

This dismissal of the serious work of rebuilding interventionist organisations that can learn to play a role in struggles and arm their members in revolutionary politics is a road to nowhere. In Macnair's case, it has done little but reproduce the sectarianism he claims to be aiming to overcome – Macnair is building an inward-looking and passive sect that loudly proclaims that only their (dubious) program of a "democratic republic" can provide the basis for successful advance.

Macnair argues that the purpose of a Marxist organisation is not to engage in small group activity, but in "high politics". But Marxists will only be able to achieve the influence necessary to impact society at this level if they pass through the hard work of individual recruitment and "activist" campaign work that Macnair derides.

Eric Blanc, an ex-revolutionary turned member of the left-liberal Democratic Socialists of America, has a clear motivation for championing Kautsky, as articulated in the pages of the reformist Jacobin Magazine: "moving away from dogmatic assumptions about the generalizability of the 1917 model should help socialists abandon other political dogmas, including on pressing issues such as how to build a

---

11. Macnair 2012.

Marxist current and whether it's okay to ever use the Democratic Party ballot line".[12]

Essentially, he argues that embracing Kautsky and erasing the divide between reformist and revolutionary strategies will free socialists up to abandon more political principles and operate "flexibly". For Blanc, this means committing wholeheartedly to the project of building a "left wing" in the thoroughly conservative and bourgeois Democratic Party. The fruits of this project, described by Blanc as an "electoral upsurge" is the election of a small layer of political hacks like Alexandria Ocasio-Cortez, whose wholehearted embrace of Biden and Harris' imperialist and anti-worker agenda would make even the most cynical Young Labor hack in Australia blush.

Greene outlines Blanc's rapid rush to the right since his embrace of "Kautskyist" politics, from entertaining the "tactical" use of the Democratic ballot line in 2017, in order to build a mass base for socialist politics, to embracing the new generation of liberal Democrats elected in the 2018 midterms, to calling for socialists to "get out the vote" for Biden in 2020. Blanc's orientation to the Democratic Party, which was initially justified as a short-term tactical expedient, is now a permanent political orientation – one which, if unchallenged, will permanently subordinate the American left to the most aggressive and successful capitalist party on the planet.

This political practice is a million miles to the right of the version of Kautsky that Blanc claims to uphold. Before the First World War, Kautsky at least claimed that workers' political independence, rejection of support for capitalist parties and refusal to participate in coalition governments were cornerstones of Marxist principle. At the same time, Blanc is methodologically a pure Kautskyist, attempting to ply formulas that are acceptable to both rightward-moving socialists and the Biden administration.

This trajectory is proof that the political demarcations drawn in Kautsky's era are still important reference points today. World War I was a decisive moment because it created the possibility of workers' revolution and clarified a division that was fundamental – socialists

---

12. Blanc 2019.

had to declare for or against cooperation with the capitalist state, for or against imperialist war, and for or against the reality of social revolution. Douglas Greene's book shows that these formative debates still echo more than a century later, as we enter a new period of polarisation and capitalist crisis.

References

Blanc, Eric 2019, "Why Kautsky Was Right (and Why You Should Care)" *Jacobin*, 2 April. https://jacobin.com/2019/04/karl-kautsky-democratic-socialism-elections-rupture

Engels, Frederick 1891, "On the 20th Anniversary of the Paris Commune [Postscript]". https://www.marxists.org/archive/marx/works/1871/civil-war-france/postscript.htm

LeBlanc, Paul 2020, "Rosa Luxemburg and the Final Conflict", *Spectre Journal*, April. https://spectrejournal.com/rosa-luxemburg-and-the-final-conflict/

Lenin, Vladimir Ilyich 1915, "Socialism and War". https://www.marxists.org/archive/lenin/works/1915/s-w/index.htm

Macnair, Mike 2010, *Revolutionary Strategy*, November Publications. https://ouleft.org/wp-content/uploads/Macnair-Revolutionary-Strategy.pdf

Macnair, Mike 2020, "End the cycle of splits" *Weekly Worker*, 23 May. https://weeklyworker.co.uk/worker/915/end-the-cycle-of-splits/

Macnair, Mike 2020, "Programmeless liquidationism", *Weekly Worker*, 8 October. https://weeklyworker.co.uk/worker/1318/programmeless-liquidationism/#fnref2

Mandel, Ernest 1978, *From Stalinism to Eurocommunism: The Bitter Fruits of "Socialism in One Country"*, Verso.

Marx, Karl 1871, "The Character of the Commune", in *The Civil War in France (First Draft)*. https://marxengels.public-archive.net/en/ME1511en_d1.html

Post, Charlie 2019, "The 'Best' of Karl Kautsky Isn't Good Enough", *Jacobin*, 3 September. https://jacobin.com/2019/03/karl-kautsky-socialist-strategy-german-revolution

MATT LAIDLAW

Review: The hidden history of revolutionary politics in Africa

Matt Laidlaw is a socialist based in Melbourne.

Revolutionary Movements in Africa: An Untold Story, edited by Pascal Bianchini, Ndongo Samba Sylla and Leo Zeilig, Pluto Press.

REVOLUTIONARY MOVEMENTS IN Africa: An Untold Story unearths the buried history of revolutionary activists and theorists who sought to go beyond the limits of the postcolonial African states. The editors note in the introduction that the "history of the revolutionary left movements in Africa is largely ignored and disregarded". Rather, histories have seen the "anti-colonial movements and radical organisations within these movements as...Soviet proxies rather than independent actors", leading to a situation where "the African continent might appear unfavourable terrain for revolutionary struggle" (p.2).

Revolutionary Movements in Africa aims to dispel that myth and bring to the light the existence of radical figures and organisations that built struggles not just opposed to "Western imperial domination" but also "against 'bureaucratised' states claiming to stand for socialism" (p.7). The 1960s and '70s are the time period most looked into, when a new revolutionary left was emerging among the postcolonial states. *Revolutionary Movements in Africa* stands as a testimony to activists of the time who, despite all the political limitations and challenges, sought to develop a revolutionary left on the continent.

The editors' collection of interviews and records of those in the struggle for a really liberated Africa is the culmination of years of research. These histories make the case that socialism did not just mean championing authoritarian regimes, but instead was a living, breathing politics inspiring the imaginations and determination of a new generation of activists. In short, the argument is that socialists who fought the new postcolonial regimes *existed*. For the socialist movement this is a history worth celebrating and drawing inspiration from today.

The editors argue that the history of the African left in the twentieth century broadly fits into three distinct periods. The initial period was marked by the majority of the African left finding themselves among the diaspora, which meant many of the radicals of the period had little direct impact on the struggles of the early twentieth century. The second phase was when the left found itself rooted in the struggles at home in the later years of colonial rule, cementing themselves as key leaders or participants in the various national struggles. These first two periods cover history far more familiar to those on the left, and this is usually where the story ends.

Revolutionary Movements in Africa, however, aims to cover the third period, a context where the revolutionaries had to adapt to new political challenges posed by the emergence of postcolonial ruling classes, struggles under those new regimes and a new relationship with imperialist powers.

Each chapter in this book covers a different political movement, spanning from Liberia to Niger, South Sudan, Madagascar and Congo-Brazzaville, among many others. Some of these chapters are from participants in the movements. Varied as the countries covered were, the political responses from the movements varied more: from peasant guerrillas in Chad, to student radicals in Tanzania and Congo-Brazzaville, socialist-unionists in Nigeria, Burkina Faso and Mali, militant high schoolers in Madagascar, brave mine workers in Namibia and even an infamous Greek-Mozambican anarchist-communist, to name a few. It is an eclectic mix of activists, with political worldviews a revolutionary socialist would also have disagreements with. Yet the recognition that student radicals, who criticised and organised against the new regimes, or that oppositional labour movements existed has all but been wiped from the historical record. This is not simply due to the blindness of mainstream history, but a deliberate erasure by the left's historians, obsessed as they are with defending the so-called socialist regimes, such as that of Julius Nyerere in Tanzania for example.

The examples of radicals organising in the post-independence world demonstrated that the revolutionary left had more to offer the workers and oppressed of Africa than authoritarian states. These movements varied from challenging aspects of the new regimes' rule to forcing revolutionaries to develop a new worldview capable of challenging the whole system.

However, the case studies in *Revolutionary Movements in Africa* are relatively sober about the serious challenges these new revolutionaries faced and how they failed to build a political alternative capable of achieving true liberation.

For starters, the revolutionary socialist left was at the absolute margins of society globally. Stalinism had been ascendant for decades, and by the 1960s and '70s was only just being challenged. For African leftists, decades of Stalinist hegemony on the left and an ascendant nationalist politics proved to be major barriers to a genuine socialist politics being developed.

The Stalinists argued that socialists must see their own developing bourgeoisie come to power, at any price, thanks to a vision of socialism that saw socialism being granted from on high. This meant that where the Stalinists were influential, they argued to the workers and the poor of their new nation to settle for what was acceptable to a new, unstable, and sometimes quickly unpopular ruling class. They argued that socialism has to wait, a national revolution comes first, there needs to be a period of unadulterated capitalist growth before your dreams of a classless society can be realised. Those who proclaimed to be "socialist" without being Stalinist, like Alphonse Massamba-Débat in the Republic of Congo, found it easy to give a socialistic language to nothing more than state-led development, while the most radical elements still clung to this top-down view of radical change. This became a consistent challenge to the emerging new revolutionaries.

In short, the old Stalinist politics, despite the potential of national movements that destabilised and kicked out world empires, wound up being the left flank of home-grown authoritarian regimes. Consequently, by distorting socialism to mean merely a top-down state-directed economy, these authoritarian leaders could present themselves as the true heroes of African socialism, with little pushback. The new generation of revolutionaries jostled against this rigid, ahistorical and conservative set of politics.

This is where *Revolutionary Movements Across Africa* becomes an indispensable resource for those who fight for a socialist world defined by working-class self-rule and total human liberation.

For the new revolutionaries, confusion came in many forms as new political questions were posed. A key question was how to relate to the new postcolonial governments. The attitudes of the left towards these governments depended a lot on their alignment towards the US or USSR, or "socialist" rhetoric. Alignment with the Soviet camp, or proclaiming to be ruling a socialist society, was often enough for much of the left to accept it as fact. However, as demonstrated in chapter 12, with the example of Julius Nyerere's government, new radicals were capable of seeing through this façade.

Governments like Nyerere's in Tanzania claimed to be running a classless society, and espousing an "African socialism". Nyerere was no Stalinist, but saw the appeal of a state-led development model in an incredibly backward country. Chapter 12 details the example of the radical Tanzanian students of the University Students African Revolutionary Front (USARF) and their struggles for a liberated Tanzania. USARF was originally established by enthusiastic radicals to champion the supposedly socialist ideals of President Julius Nyerere, through being a critical but supportive pressure group. Its formation in 1967 at the University of Dar Es Salaam, a focal point for the continent's revolutionary left, came about after the initial years of Nyerere's rule. By this point he had already proved to be a friend of the British, and a pro-capitalist warrior – violently putting down rebellions in Zanzibar and the capital, Dar Es Salaam, with the help of the British whom he pleaded with to send military aid.

As the radicals of USARF attempted to put this critical but

supportive focus into practice, they began to consciously break with the politics of Nyerere and his party, the Tanganyika African National Union. They criticised Nyerere's *Ujamaa* program – an argument for a "socialism" based on state-run collectivised agricultural production and belief that a "socialist" mindset was inherent to Africans – as "utopian". Importantly, they also stressed that Nyerere was wrong to call for socialism through cross-class unity, which was present in his plans for *Ujamaa*. For the radicals of USARF, socialism was "international and scientific", and they began to recognise that class struggle was still present in postcolonial Tanzania, which Nyerere would deny.

While this did not lead them to an immediate critique of the prevailing pro-Soviet politics of the era, they stridently opposed the idea that Nyerere presided over a classless society as he claimed. USARF engaged with Marxist theory of the past and other radicals of the day to develop their own political theory. Their critiques of Nyerere provided far more insight into the political challenges of the time than the many left academics who have written glowing reports of Nyerere's regime.

For USARF, the question of politics was also never far from the question of political organisation. While these students proved that the new period of struggle inspired some to strive for a clearer set of politics, tragically USARF spent much of their early energy meeting with and appealing to Nyerere, with some hopes they could transform his outlook to that of a true socialist. As they developed they began to see themselves as a "vanguard" organisation to lead the working class to socialist revolution, but seemingly lacked influence to act on this. USARF would only exist for three years; they were brutally repressed by the government as they increasingly became an outright opposition, leaving behind their radical magazine *Cheche*. While serious steps were beginning to be made, unfortunately nothing lasting was left behind. Nyerere is still venerated today, and the radicals of USARF largely forgotten.

A similar challenge was posed in Congo-Brazzaville, under the Massamba-Débat regime discussed in chapter 8 of the book. Massamba-Débat came to power after a general strike in Brazzaville, the capital of the Republic of Congo, overthrew the first independent government. A new layer of youth radicals sought to force the direction of the new government into a socialist one. One of their most notable achievements was forcing Massamba-Débat to accept Brazzaville becoming a refuge for the region's radicals – particularly radicals from the ex-French colonies of Gabon and Cameroon, with whose regimes the Congolese government wanted to remain on friendly terms. The youth radicals however had an elitist approach to politics, with little connection to the working class that had brought the government to power, and this limited their ability to fight for the radical changes they wanted. Massamba-Débat's regime eventually collapsed due to a coup in 1968, and then a section of the youth radicals attempted a coup of their own a few years later. Looking to figures in the military, or even believing socialism could come about through the leadership of an enlightened minority, were consistent problems across the continent.

With colonial powers being forced to leave, a new set of questions about imperialism arose for the African left: Who really rules this country? What is the relationship to the former colonial power? Chapter 13 discusses the history of University of Dar Es Salaam, with the debates over "neocolonialism" demonstrating that these questions, and who you identified as the "ruling class" of your own nation, had a political impact on the movements you built. The major political questions about the nature of the new African bourgeoisie, how to challenge imperialism in the continent and what layers are to be seen as revolutionary were all hot topics of discussion.

That few of the activists of this period came into the struggle with a clear understanding that the nationalist leaders were enemies of true liberation was to the detriment of the potential of the moment. In the popular radical literature of the time, one of the few to appreciate this dynamic was Frantz Fanon. His famous final work, *Wretched of the Earth*, makes a scathing criticism of the in-built conservatism of the rising bourgeoisie, and is a warning to his comrades to be prepared to fight them. Unfortunately, that warning is hardly the content the book is remembered for. Fanon himself was a contradictory figure who tragically never built the kind of political movement needed to challenge the enemy he identified.

Apart from this book however, much of the popular appraisals are apologies for or downright glorifications of the strategy of looking to the new postcolonial states and their state leaders as steps towards socialism, or already there. Marxists with a history of organising working-class action, like Walter Rodney, at times were not immune to such illusions in the "socialist" regimes. These at best represented a "socialism" with its soul torn asunder, filling the hole of the agency of the working class and the self-activity of the oppressed with illusions in the "progressive" role the rising petty-bourgeois African layer could play.

Softness on their new governments was not the only issue our side reckoned with. Those who broke with the older set of Stalinised and conservative nationalist politics did not immediately formulate a different worldview. Many continued to carry some version of pro-Soviet politics. For others Maoism became the next logical step. It make sense that, in a continent where several of the national movements were won through guerrilla wars and some of the key political players were military officers or a tiny group of elite students, Maoism would have an appeal.

But Maoism, where it developed among students, military officers or peasant revolutionaries, also failed the test. The Maoists found themselves unable to appeal to the rapidly urbanising populations, nor to present the movement with a power capable of properly rivalling the new ruling class. The Maoists who initiated the Derg regime in Ethiopia[1] found themselves brutally crushing the union movement there. In most places though they struggled to find a foothold.

For many activists, the influence of Maoism manifested in the belief that revolution could come from a small revolutionary elite. The Movement for Justice In Africa in Liberia, discussed in chapter 6, was a key example of this. After years of democratic struggles, and gaining influence in the student and labour movements, they fatally put their hopes in a military coup. Whatever new political orientation the new radicals chose, the problem of an elitist strategy of social change was a common weakness.

Few articulated a strategy for socialist revolution that saw the

---

1. The Derg, officially known as the Provisional Military Administrative Council (PMAC) and which claimed to be "Marxist-Leninist", was the military dictatorship that ruled Ethiopia from 1974 to 1991.

working class as leaders. The lack of a tradition of revolutionary socialist politics made it an incredibly tall order for activists to draw all the necessary lessons of the failure of the various socialist, communist and national parties to liberate the mass of people. It also related to the class many of the revolutionaries came from, which was a privileged middle class, often students. These radicals took the first steps, but were cut short by a mix of their own shortcomings and the brutal crushing of their organisations.

Marxism, with its focus on revolutionary class struggle as the only way to liberate the world from capitalism, was argued to be Eurocentric, and inapplicable to the countries of Africa, with its far smaller working classes in much more backward economies. While there is no doubt that in some countries the working class was tiny and had little strategic power, many African nations had small, but strategically powerful working classes who were active for decades preceding independence, and often more so post-independence.

Many on the left globally write off the relevance of Marxist politics to struggles across Africa, arguing that it is a politics only relevant to the *particular* class structures and history of Europe and the industrial world. Yet reading about the radical struggles of this period, it is hard to accept the legitimacy of this argument.

The example of Nigeria in chapter 5, with its radical student milieu and powerful working class, refutes the idea that Marxist politics did not match with reality in the African context. Immediately after World War II, returned soldiers and industrial workers struck for an increase in the cost-of-living-allowance, crippling the British governorate. This power to shake the foundations of the colonial regime inspired the newly forming radical "Zikist" students. Named after a particularly conservative nationalist, Nnamdi Azikiwe, the students quickly broke from his flawed strategy and began to see the need for the organised working class to play a key role in the fight against British imperialism. Socialist unionists became part of the political leadership of the national liberation movement. They presented a terrifying threat to the British, who moved to divide and rule politics – establishing structural divisions in government along regional lines in the 1947 constitution. Then the 1951 constitution gave further power to the various ethnic and regional leaders through federalisation and training a new layer of trusted "natives" to take over running the state when the British would grant formal independence. While the movement failed the challenge of federalism, which has defined Nigerian politics since, the postwar period showed that the organised working class could lead radical students and the poor across the country. Unfortunately, socialist parties built around those politics were small, or incredibly new, and tended to fracture. The succeeding decades post-independence have seen the same dynamic play out over and over in Nigeria: the latent power of the working class, sometimes mobilised, sometimes successful against even military regimes, but lacking an organised socialist leadership.

Through the early post-independence years, we see the frequent flourishing of an enthusiastic, hopeful generation of activists continuing their fight for liberation. While politically confused about their allies and enemies, they fought. Many of the first to take those steps were from the generation of relatively privileged university and high school students. The book gives a wonderful account of the defiant Madagascan high schoolers, whose constant striking brought down their first independent government. Elsewhere, like in Congo-Brazzaville, it is the youth wing of the new ruling parties that has proven a thorn in the side of the regime as they try to carry out the promises of liberation for the *entire* continent already reneged on by their party leaders.

The contradiction of a wave of revolutions fighting for a vague but inspiring total transformation of life for the masses of Africa, but not seeing much of the change promised, provided ample fuel for radicals. Much like across Europe and America, the new generation of activists, young and many from the expanding student population, gave a political dynamism and militancy that had the potential to sweep aside the crusted, old leaders. That they politically failed to fully capitalise on this moment does not take away from its potential.

Additionally, in many of the examples, such as Nigeria, Mali and Burkina Faso, the working class became a key problem for the new regimes' ability to enforce their rule. It had been the constant union agitation in Burkina Faso that had created the space for Thomas

Sankara[2] to push for power, and it should be seared into the mind of every revolutionary that thousands of teachers struck, were sacked and had their union destroyed by the Sankara regime. Any socialist movement must be built off these heroes' amazing struggles, not champion the leaders who saw the working-class struggle as a thorn in their side. The tragedy that is the reality of this period is that our side was too *confused, small and disorganised* to make good on the potential of the period.

Thanks to Bianchini, Sylla and Zeilig and the many others who contributed their experiences and histories there is now more evidence of the potential of these movements, and the relevance of revolutionary politics. Armed with some information long disappeared from the public record, held only by the few living activists of the various movements, revolutionaries should feel emboldened to argue that a revolutionary Marxist politics has as much to offer to the oppressed in Africa as it has elsewhere in the world. The book promises there are more case studies to be uncovered, from which revolutionaries are sure to draw lessons and inspiration. If the dream of a truly liberated Africa, and the world at large, is to be realised, these histories should be taken seriously.

---

2. Thomas Sankara was a military officer who was inspired by the Cuban revolution led by Fidel Castro and Che Guevara. He took power in a coup in 1983 and served as President of Burkina Faso until his assassination in 1987.

www.ingramcontent.com/pod-product-compliance
Lightning Source LLC
Chambersburg PA
CBHW012004090526
44590CB00026B/3868